The Prentice Hall Directory of
Online Social Studies Resources

RONALD L. PARTIN

Prentice Hall, Paramus, NJ 07652

Library of Congress Cataloging-in-Publication Data

Partin, Ronald L.
    Prentice Hall directory of online social studies resources : 1,000 of the most valuable social studies Web sites, electronic mailing lists & newsgroups / Ronald L. Partin.
        p.   cm.
    ISBN 0-13-679887-X
    1. Social sciences—Computer network resources—Directories. 2. Social sciences—Computer network resources—Reviews. 3. Internet (Computer network) in education. I. Title.
H61.95.P37   1998   97-30121
025.06'3'0025—dc21   CIP

Printed in the United States of America

10 9 8 7 6 5 4 3 2

ISBN 0-13-679887-X

 PRENTICE HALL
Paramus, NJ 07652

A Simon & Schuster Company

On the World Wide Web at http://www.phdirect.com

Prentice Hall International (UK) Limited, London
Prentice Hall of Australia Pty. Limited, Sydney
Prentice Hall Canada Inc., Toronto
Prentice Hall Hispanoamericana, S.A., Mexico
Prentice Hall of India Private Limited, New Delhi
Prentice Hall of Japan, Inc., Tokyo
Simon & Schuster Asia Pte. Ltd., Singapore
Editora Prentice Hall do Brasil, Ltda., Rio de Janeiro

Dedicated with much love
to our sons,
Matthew and Brett Partin.

ACKNOWLEDGMENTS

This project would have been much more difficult without the emotional support and encouragement of my wife Jan. The diligent efforts of Connie Kallback, Zsuzsa Neff, and the editorial and production staff at the Applied Center for Research in Education and Prentice Hall are most appreciated.

The clip art in this book was selected from a variety of electronic sources, including: *DeskTop Art* from Dynamic Graphics, *Desk Gallery* by Zedcor Corporation, *About Art: Education* by Dynamic Graphics, *Metro ImageBase*, and *Volk Clip Art* from Dynamic Graphics.

My appreciation to the hundreds of persons who created the splendid Web sites catalogued in this book. Conscientious effort was made to provide appropriate credit to the sponsors or creators of these Web sites. Please do forward any corrections or additions to the author.

ABOUT THE AUTHOR

In November of 1996, Ron Partin celebrated his 50th birthday by retiring two weeks later. He was Professor of Educational Foundations and Inquiry and Coordinator of the Guidance and Counseling Program at Bowling Green State University. As a counselor educator, he taught courses in educational consultation, group dynamics, counseling, and learning psychology. A former high school social studies teacher and coach, Ron is in demand as a speaker, trainer, and consultant and is known for facilitating interactive, fun workshops.

The author of numerous journal articles on time management, goal setting, creative problem solving, stress management, and effective teaching skills, Ron is also the co-author of *P.R.I.D.E.*, a training program on effective classroom management, which has been completed by over 50,000 teachers nationwide. He is the co-author of *The Social Studies Teacher's Survival Kit* and author of *The Social Studies Teacher's Book of Lists*, and *The Classroom Teacher's Survival Guide*, all published by Prentice Hall.

Ron and his wife, Jan, are the parents of twin sons, both now in graduate school. He has a broad range of interests, including woodworking, golf, basketball, genealogy, curling, flower gardening, bluegrass music, and making stained glass windows. His overwhelming passion continues to be helping teachers become more effective.

ABOUT THIS RESOURCE

A fourth-grade student submits a question to a researcher in Antarctica, immediately receiving the answer along with panoramic photographs of icebergs. A history teacher acquires copies of letters sent by Galutia York, a Union soldier, to his New York family during the Civil War. A North Carolina teacher exchanges ideas on teaching about racial discrimination with a teacher in Utah. Students from around the world interact in an on-line simulation of the United Nations Security Council, studying other countries and representing their assigned country as it wrestles with the challenges of maintaining world peace. Students in Ohio exchange messages with a group of children in a Bosnian refugee camp. American and Russian students have jointly published a newspaper.

These events are not the idle dreams of an academic futurist, but only a small sample of the exciting learning opportunities available today on the Internet.

The Internet presents a virtual galaxy of resources, though much time can be wasted extracting the gems from what is useless and irrelevant. This book is intended to help social studies teachers quickly locate those gems which will enrich their teaching. Many sites would be appropriate for interactive student use; thousands of others would prove valuable as supportive resources in preparing lesson plans. While it is not essential that students have access to the Internet, teachers who do have an immense storehouse of teaching resources at their fingertips. Most teachers have this access either at home or at school, or through public and university libraries.

Home computers are not only available to children from wealthy families. One recent survey found that 30% of the families with children and with incomes *under* $30,000 had a computer in their homes. An estimated nine million adults log onto the Internet daily; this is likely exceeded by the number of students. Spending on home computers now exceeds expenditures for televisions. We read of Bill Gate's investment of billions of dollars into a worldwide system of hovering satellites interconnecting any two remote points in the world with the ultimate World-Wide Web.

Many teachers are already exploring the stimulating adventures hidden in the Internet. They and their students have the power to tap into thousands of databases and original resources. Hundreds of photographs can be downloaded from sites such as the Smithsonian Museum. Teachers are able to contact other teachers and experts in their discipline to exchange ideas, locate resources, and collaborate on projects.

Many educators and futurists predict that the Internet and rapidly changing computer technology will influence not only what is taught, but also how it is taught. Thousands of classrooms are already connected in virtual communities, interacting and discussing and tackling real world problems. Enthusiasts have heralded many prior technological innovations (e.g., film, television, videorecording, programmed instruction, computers) as the panacea for education. The Internet does present tremendous opportunities for enriching learning, motivating students, and saving teachers time, but ultimately its influence on learning will be determined by the ability of individual classroom teachers to tap that rich potential. That success will require training in the use of the Internet, adequate resources and support, motivation, and creativity.

HOW THIS BOOK CAN HELP WITH YOUR TEACHING TASKS

When I first started teaching I assumed teachers had to prepare every lesson from scratch. The first night I spent six hours preparing for the next day's classes. With five preparations (American history, world history, sociology, psychology, and Advanced Placement American history), I very quickly realized this was an impossible task for even the most dedicated teacher. I soon realized that wise teachers research many sources for proven ideas and adapt successful lesson ideas and resources from colleagues, workshops, books, or journals. What a lifesaver that discovery was! Of course, preparing five lesson plans a day was still a challenge the first few years, but it became a whole lot easier once I learned to tap the creative resources around me.

While professional journals and books, curriculum workshops, and face-to-face mentors are still valuable assets, the Internet can be a great supplement for beginning, as well as for experienced teachers.

This book should be of value to both the "Newbie" (Internet lingo for beginner) and advanced users because both social studies teachers and student teachers can tap the creativity of other teachers.

ASSUMPTIONS

Two basic assumptions guided the construction of this book:

▲ You already possess basic understanding of how to use a computer. It is not necessary to be a technophile. Just the basics will do: turn the computer on, open files, and call up a browser, such as Netscape. You can drive a car quite well without knowing a thing about fuel injectors, or operate a CD player without understanding how it performs its magic. This book is not intended as a basic tutorial on the Internet. If you need help with the basic tasks of getting connected to the Internet, setting up a browser, or using search engines, please refer to any of the excellent books and online tutorials listed in the Appendix.

▲ You have access to a computer connected to the Internet and World-Wide Web. It doesn't matter whether you are using a Macintosh or PC, as long as you can access the Internet. From home, and from most schools, this will also require a modem. If you are planning to purchase a modem, don't buy anything less than a 28,800 bps modem. The cost savings for anything less are insignificant and you will spend more time waiting for graphics-laden Web pages to load. Most libraries now provide Internet access, as does a growing number of schools.

SPECIAL FEATURES

A full section is devoted to each of the major subjects included in social studies. The bulk of these listings is comprised of Web sites and the Internet addresses necessary for easy access. Listings of newsgroups and discussion groups will also be provided for each subject area so that teachers may directly contact experts and professionals in practically every topic taught in the social studies domain.

Resources for learning more about the Internet and a glossary of Internet-related terms are included at the end of the book.

This book provides a gold mine of the best teaching resources on the Internet. True, you could find these sites yourself, if you could afford to spend hours browsing the thousands of social studies related sites on the Internet. For the teachers who just don't have that much discretionary time, I have invested hundreds of hours extracting the gems from thousands of useless, biased, poorly constructed, inaccurate, or blatantly commercial Web sites. For every one site included in this listing dozens were discarded as inappropriate. Be aware, of course, thousands of new documents come online each day.

CRITERIA FOR INCLUDING WEB SITES

How does one select the best Web sites from among the millions of documents available? This would prove an overwhelming task without a set of criteria to guide the selection process. Persons weighting the same criteria differently or using different ones may well come up with a different pool. These are the guidelines used in picking the best of the best for inclusion in this directory.

▲ Relevancy—Many sites are very interesting, charming, entertaining, or even amusing, but really not of much apparent value in teaching social studies. Even those which had worthwhile academic content were more suited to the needs of teachers from disciplines other than social studies.

▲ Adequacy of coverage—Does the source add anything beyond what is already in most high school textbooks? Most of the sites examined did not. They were often colorful encyclopedia articles, with perhaps a few links to other sources. Probably most non-commercial sites, including personal home pages, are little more than lists of favorite links. Often these lists crosslist each other, putting the unsuspecting user into a perpetual "cybercycle."

▲ Credibility of the source — Just as content from books, tabloid magazines, and television talk shows is often uncritically passed along as "fact," Internet content must be skeptically scrutinized for the same reason. Indeed, the anonymity of the Internet makes it easier to pawn inaccurate, misleading, and outright falsehoods as truth. Anyone with access to a computer and Internet connection can construct a Web page. Even without malicious intent, a lot of garbage ends up posted on the Net. Flashy professionally drawn graphics are easy to add, giving an undeserved aura of legitimacy. "Who says so?" is the first question to ask in assessing the credibility of any source. The name of the sponsor or creator is included with each of the Web site citations in the book.

▲ Timeliness of information—How recently was the site updated? One great benefit of the Internet is the rapidity with which information can be shared. News can appear almost instantaneously, while it will take hours to reach the newspapers, days or perhaps weeks to find its way into journals and magazines, and even months to be published in a book. Items may have been accurate when they were posted on the Net three years ago, yet outdated now.

▲ Readability—Is the text well-written, with a minimum of grammatical and typographical errors? Is the site filled with technical jargon? Some sites which look promising at first are really intended for content specialists, often in a very esoteric field.

▲ Navigability—How difficult is it to move around the pages within the Web site? Does the user have to guess what to do next? User-friendliness in a Web site is a real bonus.

▲ Use of media—Some sites have splashy graphics, video or clips ("eye candy" in Net jargon) which add nothing to their academic value and consume inordinate amounts of time loading onto your computer. Fluff sites with little to offer have been avoided. On the other hand, totally text-reliant sources are little more than books on a computer screen. Effective use of audio clips, relevant instructions, and color backgrounds can make the site more appealing.

▲ Convenience—Some sites which might have worthwhile content have been eliminated because they require a specialized set of browser plug-ins to function or were overloaded with large graphics, requiring long periods of waiting to load. Unless the content that finally arrived was valuable, these sites were not included. When they were, a note has been made that the site may take a bit longer than normal to load.

READING THE DIRECTORY

For ease of use, the directory has been organized into sections corresponding to the basic social studies course titles. While there could be other ways to cluster the hundreds of Web sites, the generic course headings are still most universally understood by social studies teachers. Of course, many Web sites contained resources which might be valuable in more than one social studies area (e.g., sociology and world history). A subjective judgment had to be made as to where the bulk of the content would best fit. It would probably be worthwhile to browse even those social studies subject areas you do not teach for useful materials.

The site title or subject appears in the first line, followed on the second line by the URL (Uniform Resource Locator), which tells the computer where to find the specific file and what kind of application it will be. In the world of computers, there is no partial credit; you must type the URL precisely as it appears or the file will not be opened. Following the description of the Web resource, the site's creator or sponsor is included in brackets [ ].

Every effort has been made to assure that all URLs are correct and current. In the rapidly changing world of the Internet, however, it is inevitable that some sites will move or become discontinued. If you should receive an error message that no such URL exists, please attempt the following steps:

1. Carefully retype the URL exactly as it appears in this book and try again.
2. If the retyped address still does not work, enter the title of the Web site into a search engine, such as AltaVista. Three or four keywords may be sufficient in most cases. It is more likely that a number of "hits" will be posted. Scroll through the first few to see if the site you are seeking is listed. Don't waste time reading through hundreds of listings.
3. Try submitting the name of the sponsor or creator of the Web page. It will be listed in brackets at the end of the site's directory entry.
4. Check our Web site at http://www.teachersbookshelf.com for updates of the social studies directory.
5. If you still have no success, please contact me <rpartin@bgnet.bgsu.edu> describing the site you are having difficulty locating.

SEARCH ENGINES

A quick way to locate Internet documents on a particular topic is to use a "search engine." This is an online application which uses key words or phrases you enter to conduct a search of literally millions of documents.

AltaVista purports to be the largest search service, accessed over 29 million times per weekday. It claims users can access over 31 million pages found on 476,000 servers, and four million articles from 14,000 USENET newsgroups.

ZRsearch contains five of the most common search engines: Yahoo!, Lycos, Magellan, WebCrawler, and a shareware index (Shareware.com). http.//www.zrhome.com/iwc/search.html.

CONTENTS

About the Author   v
About this Resource   vi

Section 1

THE INTERNET AS AN EDUCATIONAL RESOURCE   1

What Is the Internet?   2
The World Wide Web   2
The Internet in Education   3
How Teachers Are Using the Internet   3
Student E-Mail Exchanges   4
Communicating with Knowledgeable Persons   5
Telementoring   5
Online Expeditions   6
Student Collaborations   7
Student Web Page Projects   7
Accessing Data from Remote Sites   8
Virtual Museums and Exhibits   9
Examples of Educational Use of the Internet   10
Online Courses   10
Newsgroups   11
Newsgroup Prefixes   13
Mailing Lists   15
Monitoring Student Use of the Internet   16
Copyright Restrictions   16

Section 2

GENERAL SOCIAL STUDIES RESOURCES   18

Best Web Sites   19
Electronic Mailing Lists   23
Education Newsgroups   27

Section 3

AMERICAN HISTORY   28

Best Web Sites   29
Electronic Mailing Lists   62
Newsgroups   64

Section 4

WORLD HISTORY **65**

  Best Web Sites 66
  Electronic Mailing Lists 90
  Newsgroups 93

Section 5

CONSUMER ECONOMICS **95**

  Best Web Sites 96
  Electronic Mailing Lists 116
  Newsgroups 117

Section 6

SOCIOLOGY **118**

  Best Web Sites 119
  Electronic Mailing Lists 133
  Electronic Journals 138
  Newsgroups 138

Section 7

PSYCHOLOGY **140**

  Best Web Sites 141
  Electronic Mailing Lists 160
  Newsgroups 163

Section 8

GEOGRAPHY **166**

  Best Web Sites 167
  Electronic Mailing Lists 188
  Newsgroups 191

Section 9

AMERICAN GOVERNMENT **192**

  Best Web Sites 193
  Electronic Mailing Lists 211
  Newsgroups 214

Section 10

CURRENT EVENTS **216**

  Best Web Sites 217
  Online Newspapers 232
  Electronic Mailing Lists 236
  Newsgroups 239

APPENDIX   *240*

    Online Beginner's Guides to Using the Internet   241
    Books on Using the Internet   244
    Glossary of Common Internet Terms   244
        Reading Domain Suffixes   245
    Internet Slang and Conventions   247
        Common Emoticons   248

THE INTERNET AS AN EDUCATIONAL RESOURCE

Since 1995 more mail has been handled by the Internet than by the U.S. Post Office. The "information superhighway" has become one of the hottest topics of the 90s. It is virtually impossible to pick up a current newspaper or magazine without encountering at least one article on the Internet. In his 1997 inaugural address, President Clinton made six references to the Internet and urged a national commitment to connect every student in America by the year 2000. Many states have already made this commitment with the result that thousands of schools are already wired into the information superhighway.

In truth, few trends since the advent of television have engendered such enthusiastic and rapid growth as the Internet. One in ten Americans logs on at least once a week; nine million adults do so each day. MCI estimates that Internet traffic increases by 30% each month. An estimated 300 million people worldwide will be connected by 1999 and 1.5 billion by 2001. Over 500,000 Web sites (accessible computer databases) currently exist, doubling every six months. Over 10,000 Usenet (discussion) groups exist online, creating a community bulletin board for virtually every conceivable human interest or specialty. The prospect of a worldwide network of 300 hovering satellites will make the Internet accessible from every location on Earth, without the need for land-lines.

WHAT IS THE INTERNET?

The Internet is a complex worldwide labyrinth of thousands of interconnected computer networks. Its origin can be traced to the Arpanet, developed in the early 1970s by the U.S. Defense Department. It incorporated a set of protocols, or "rules of the road," which facilitate computers on a network communicating with each other. In the late 1980s, the National Science Foundation sponsored an experimental network, connecting university researchers with the National Science Foundation's supercomputers via telephone lines. The NSFnet, as this new high-speed network became known, grew to interconnect colleges and universities with the supercomputer sites and each other.

Originally it was the domain of academics and a few technophiles; then the advent of Internet providers such as America Online and CompuServe made Internet access widely available to the general population. Soon many students were "surfing" the "Net," often tutoring their teachers on how to navigate this new resource.

THE WORLD WIDE WEB

In 1992, the advent of the World Wide Web (usually just shortened to "the Web" or WWW) by the European Particle Physics Laboratory (CERN) dramatically popularized the Internet by suddenly making it user-friendly. In its early days, users had to type a long URL address for each specific file, far from a user-friendly process. The WWW adapted a computer language (HTML) based on a software convention called hypertext. When a text item is clicked, the computer zips to another Web site, which may be located on a computer thousands of miles away. A single page of text could contain dozens of links to as many different Web sites.

Use of the Internet escalated with the introduction of browsers, such as Netscape, which incorporated "point and click" navigation of the growing number of Internet sites. Hypermedia incorporated not only hypertext, but also sounds, graphic images, and even movies. Of course, the latter require much larger files, longer time to load onto a user's computer, and faster computers with more internal memory.

THE INTERNET IN EDUCATION

Many of the millions of Web sites are useless or irrelevant for school use by either students or teachers. Although originally designed as an academic communications tool, the Internet's phenomenal growth has come largely with the rush by businesses to add commercial sites. With a minimal investment any organization or individual can have immediate access to a worldwide market for its ideas or products. Today over 50% of the Web sites are commercial ventures, seeking to sell their wares through this relatively inexpensive marketing tool. The Internet presents a virtual galaxy of resources, though much time can be wasted sorting the gems from the useless and irrelevant resources. This book is intended to help social studies teachers quickly locate those resources which will enrich their teaching.

Students having access to the Internet have truly joined the global community. Previously unmotivated students often become enthusiastic about the real-world challenges and resources it makes available. It also offers great promise as an instrument of collaboration. Many teachers and students have found creative, exciting ways to collaborate using the powers of Cyberspace technology to explore new challenges.

Teachers and students have used the Internet to meet and work with experts, writers, scientists, politicians, and other professionals. In so doing they can tap the richness of the real-world resources firsthand, applying their classroom learning to the broader community and the world of work. Of course, such interactions with professionals could become a nuisance to the professionals with little educational benefit to the students if done without the guidance and training of effective teachers.

Teachers have also begun to tap the potential of the Internet for professional development, school reform, and curriculum improvement, as well as for its rich archives of lesson plans, student activities, course syllabi, and other instructional aids.

HOW TEACHERS ARE USING THE INTERNET

Probably not since the introduction of the printing press has a technological innovation garnered such enthusiasm from the educational community. Sure, some hype can oversell the merits of the information superhighway. The Internet is but another tool at the teacher's disposal. Just as the printed page, chalk, movie projectors, and television proved useful, but not panaceas, the computer and Cyberspace technologies will never eliminate the teacher's job. But they will most certainly have an impact on the teacher's role. While there will be false starts and failed experiments, increased access to information and collaboration with others will surely enrich teachers' effectiveness.

A Gargantuan Virtual Library

The Internet provides instantaneous, 24-hour-a-day access to a massive collection of information about practically any topic—and it's all free or rather inexpensive. Exchange lesson ideas with social studies teachers around the world; download primary documents; retrieve "up-to-the-minute" news of world events; pick the brains of an online mentor; take virtual tours of some of the world's finest museums and exhibitions; or collaborate with experts on research projects. Every day, creative teachers and students are expanding its innovative, educational uses.

As schools gain Internet accessibility, teachers are creating individualized curriculum pages with hypertext links to the best Web sites related to the course content.

STUDENT E-MAIL EXCHANGES

One of the first classroom uses of the Internet was to permit students to exchange e-mail messages with other students around the world. One-on-one pen pal exchanges have been successfully initiated by social studies teachers since schools first gained access. While some organization and coaching of students are required to make this a maximally effective learning tool, such exchanges provide a valuable, real-world, international experience to thousands of students. In the past three years a number of organizations have undertaken the mission of matching students for e-mail correspondence.

St. Olaf College's IECC (Intercultural E-Mail Classroom Connections <http://www.stolaf.edu/network/iecc/>) matches its students with those from other cultures and countries in e-mail classroom pen-pal and project exchanges.

KIDLINK <http://www.kidlink.org/home-txt.html> (Remember not to type the < >'s.) seeks to involve students, ages 10–15, in global dialogues. Since 1990, over 60,000 kids from 87 countries have participated in a variety of collaborative activities. KIDPROJ<http://www.kidlink.org /KIDPROJ/projects.html> informs teachers of a variety of educational projects provided through the KIDLINK, dozens of which have involved students around the world. For example, the Money Project encouraged students to submit e-mail descriptions and pictures of their local currency, to share information on their country's exchange rate, and to compare what various items cost in their countries.

COMMUNICATING WITH KNOWLEDGEABLE PERSONS

An individual student submits a question to a state senator about a school funding bill under consideration. The next day the senator replies, leading to several exchanges between the two. The student shares these messages with the rest of the class. In this way, students have been successfully using the Internet e-mail as a research vehicle, exchanging messages with politicians, scientists, national leaders, and other experts.

While corresponding with world leaders and experts is not a new learning experience, the convenience (and perhaps, to a degree, the novelty) of the Internet has encouraged many students to seek the opinions and wisdom of authorities on a range of topics. No doubt busy experts could be overwhelmed by students wanting help with their homework assignments; nevertheless most do selectively respond to student inquiries because they want to be helpful, though they may be too busy to respond personally to every request.

Some training is necessary before students submit e-mail messages to experts and newsmakers. Here are a few tips to reinforce:

▲ Be very specific in making requests. It is better to ask one or two concrete questions than to make a blanket demand, such as "Send me all you have on the Supreme Court." The more specific the request the more likely it is to receive a reply.

▲ Be concise. Long wordy requests may not even be read. A brief statement of the student's identity ("I am a seventh grade student in Kalida, Ohio") preceding the question or request is appropriate and more likely to gain the receiver's attention and sympathy.

▲ Celebrities are generally less likely to reply than lesser known persons, though a well-written inquiry may sometimes catch their attention. People such as the President who receive huge volumes of mail may rely on volunteers or staff members to screen and reply to their messages.

▲ Many experts have Web pages, often with a link to their e-mail address. Almost always they will return at least brief responses to reasonable student requests.

▲ Caution students not to take it personally if a message is not answered. Explain how busy these persons are and how great the demands may be on their time.

▲ Encourage students to share their responses with classmates to extend the learning experience.

TELEMENTORING

By design or by chance these contacts often evolve into telementoring experiences, where the adult works with one or more students through the Internet connection. Volunteer online mentors can fulfill many of the same roles a face-to-face mentor could and probably with less time commitment. They not only give encouragement and serve as positive role models, but can provide students feedback on projects and ideas, link students to helpful resources, and even collaborate on research activities.

Contact in advance by the teacher requesting cooperation and explaining the concept of telementoring may improve the willingness of experts to participate in the experience. While the mentors may be located anywhere in the world, don't overlook the opportunities which may exist within the local community. Government officials, retired persons, and professionals may be quite willing to undertake this role as a new and most rewarding experience.

A World Wide Web registry <http://www.covis.nwu.edu/> has been established for scientists willing to serve as telementors. Hopefully, similar clearinghouses will develop to involve other professionals.

ONLINE EXPEDITIONS

Many students have become actively involved in online expeditions into the Mayan ruins, Antarctica, or a re-creation of Magellan's circumnavigation of the globe. By tapping the experiences of experts, explorers, or persons in unique situations, valuable real-time classroom learning is at the students' fingertips.

The MayaQuest Program is a remarkable example of the vast potential of the Internet as a learning resource. A team of bicyclists pedaled throughout Mexico, communicating via the Internet twice weekly with hundreds of students in the United States as the team visited a series of Mayan archaeological sites. The field investigators used a portable laptop computer, modem and cellular phone to transmit messages, answer questions, and send digitized photos of their adventure. One significant archaeological discovery was broadcast live to students, months before it would appear in the professional journals and years before it would be published in any textbook. The students studied the data sent by the archaeologists and voted on which site the team should visit next.

"TerraQuest" has become a front-runner in the organization of the online educational expeditions. Using digital technology, photographs are processed in the field and loaded onto the TerraQuest Web page via satellite so that users can follow the day-to-day progress. Three exceptional expeditions have been logged thus far: a climb up Yosemite National Park's "El Capitan," a tour of the beauty and wildlife of Virtual Galápagos, and a polar exploration through Virtual Antarctica.

The "Follow Us" project permitted some 300 schools around the world to track two explorers as they became the first to ski, unaided, to the North Pole. Students from Confederation High School in Ottawa, Canada, ran an Internet site with an e-mail connection to the pair of explorers as they trekked the frozen tundra. This team of 50 students relayed about 60 e-mail messages each day from the other schools to the explorers via satellite. The students then relayed the responses back.

Everyone involved learned more about the Arctic in this marvelous example of the educational potential of the Internet.

Each year, the "Jason Project," led by Dr. Robert D. Ballard, undertakes a two-week scientific exploration in a remote area of the world. Live, interactive Internet broadcasts permit students around the world to follow the progress of the expedition. Previous years' online projects have included: Journey from the Center of the Earth; Field Study: Bird Populations; Aquatic Field Study; and Novel Talks. Videotapes and curriculum materials from past expeditions are available for purchase. An excellent set of lessons, activities, and downloadable maps enable teachers to facilitate the learning process. The "Teacher Forum" discussion group permits teachers to exchange instructional ideas about these projects.

Magellan Global Adventure and Trindade Now 96 sponsored the first e-sail adventure as the Schurmann family crew visited exotic places en route to re-creating Ferdinand Magellan's circumnavigation of the world. Satellite transmission of video clips put student adventurers at the helm of this exciting expedition.

Each of the above online expeditions is described in the Web site listings in this book. Many others are likely to be developed in the future.

STUDENT COLLABORATIONS

The National Geographic Society sponsors Kids Network, a collaborative project involving students in working on real-world problems. They collaborate with their classmates as well as with a research team composed of ten or more classes from schools around the world. The project includes schools in 44 countries and every continent except Antarctica. Most exchanges are in English, though the English of some international participants may be limited.

Thousands of schools in 25 countries are connected to I*EARN (the International Education and Resource Network), a global communication network allowing students to collaborate on an assortment of problems. Many students participated in the Water Project, collecting local water samples and exchanging data with other schools.

The Youth In Action Network <http://www.mightymedia.com/youth> encourages students and teachers worldwide to become engaged in social action to protect the environment and human rights.

During the spring floods of 1997, students in Minnesota and Wisconsin posted daily reports and photographs on the Rivers of Life: Mississippi Adventure Web site <http://elsie.hamline.edu/rivers>.

STUDENT WEB PAGE PROJECTS

Many teachers now permit students to create Internet Web pages as part of their course learning package. As a hands-on instructional tool, the use of the Internet can be a powerful motivator. Many of the most creative educational Web pages have been developed by students, even many of elementary age, as classroom projects. This option provides many benefits:

▲ The use of Web page construction projects has a high interest level, motivating even the most reluctant learners.

▲ Designed as a cooperative learning activity, such projects can encourage student collaboration.

▲ Other students, as well as adults, worldwide, have access to the Web project, potentially reaching a broader audience than more traditional projects.

▲ Seeing the products of their efforts used by others can be a great source of pride for the students and provide positive visibility for their schools.

▲ With the national trend toward portfolio assessment, Web page design provides a valuable alternative mode of assessing student learning.

For a glimpse of the educational potential of using Web page construction as a part of the social studies curriculum, check out some the following student-designed Web sites:

Life in the Middle Ages
http://www.burbank.k12.ca.us/~luther/midages/beginhere.html

Currency Exchange and The Gang of Fifteen
http://ecedweb.unomaha.edu/gang1.htm

Design Paradise
http://ananke.advanced.org/2111/

Edustock (a stock market simulation)
http://tqd.advanced.org/3088/

Investing for Kids
http://tqd.advanced.org/3096/

Thousands of schools have set up their own Web sites, many including excellent student-designed pages. Visit Web66 <http://web66.coled.umn.edu/schools.html> for one of the most complete listings of school Web sites worldwide. By May of 1997, approximately 6,000 schools in the United States had constructed Web sites. See International Schools CyberFair 97 at <http://www.gsn.org/gsn/cb/> for over 250 student-designed school Web pages from 27 countries.

ACCESSING DATA FROM REMOTE SITES

Dozens of sites provide archives of social studies lesson plans, course syllabi, and classroom activities. The quality of these can vary, but many ideas can be gleaned from tapping these valuable resources. A few of the best lesson archives include the following:

Columbia Education Center's Mini Lessons
http://youth.net/cec/cec.html

Connections +
http://mcrel.org/connect/plus/

ERIC/ChESS (ERIC Clearinghouse for Social Studies/Social Science Education)
http://www.indiana.edu/~ssdc/eric-chess.html

Marty Levine's Lesson Plans and Resources for Social Studies Teachers

Teachers' Net Lesson Plan Exchange
http://teachers.net/lessons/

Lesson Plans and Resources for Social Studies Teachers
http://www.csun.edu/~hcedu013/index.html

The World Wide Web provides an immense virtual library with immediate access 24 hours a day to millions of documents, images, sound recordings, and movie clips. As you discover the best, use the bookmark of your browser to mark them for easy access in the future. Many outstanding archives, such as The HistoryNet: World History <http://www.thehistorynet.com>, should be checked periodically because they are updated regularly.

Information overload is a major problem confronting the Internet user. Culling the gems from the slag can consume endless hours in an already crowded schedule. Annotated guides, such as this book, can prove a valuable timesaver. With the ever-growing mass of Web sites just keeping up with the additions becomes an overwhelming task. Be sure to check the Prentice Hall Web site at http://www.teachersbookshelf.com periodically for continual updates of new sites as they are discovered. You may also suggest your favorite sites to the author by e-mail at <rpartin@bgnet.bgsu.edu>.

VIRTUAL MUSEUMS AND EXHIBITS

The World Wide Web's hypertext links permit teachers and students to control the navigation through multimedia exhibitions of text, sound recordings, movie clips, and graphic images. The interactive capabilities of the best educational Internet sites make this an active learning medium rather than one in which students only participate as passive observers. For an excellent sampling of the finest online exhibitions, check Best Web Museums and Tours <http://www.lightlink.com/steve/>.

Many real museums, like the Smithsonian, develop online exhibits which incorporate a portion of their special exhibits. Other virtual museums exist only in Cyberspace, linking a collage of resources into an online collection. This concept has tremendous potential and will probably grow in the future.

Some schools have established their own virtual museums. Students research a concept and develop a Web site, collecting a set of related resources in a virtual exhibit. Done well, developing virtual tours, museums, or exhibits as a collaborative class project can be not only a great motivational tool, but can also enhance learning and cooperative work skills.

EXAMPLES OF EDUCATIONAL USE OF THE INTERNET

For a sampling of ideas on how teachers are adapting the Internet and World Wide Web for creative, educational uses, check the following sites:

k-12 Internet Testbed Project

http://www.nylink.org/testbed/projdescrip.html

Educational Hotlist

http://www.fi.edu/tfi/hotlists/kid-hist.html

Our Home

http://ellesmere.ccm.emr.ca/ourhome/

Peto's Class Student Projects

http://www.owt.com/phs/classrooms/peto/stu.html

ONLINE COURSES

The number of interactive courses available on the Internet is growing daily. While most are designed for post-secondary students, many could be used as well by advanced high school students. Others can provide teachers with valuable lesson ideas. For current information on the array of online courses available on the World Wide Web, check the following sites:

Globewide Network Academy

http://cgi.gnacademy.org:1089/cgibin/frontpage.cgi

International Centre for Distance Learning (ICDL)

http://www-icdl.open.ac.uk/

Internet University

http://www.caso.com/

Teaching and Learning on the Web

http://www.mcli.dist.maricopa.edu/tl/

World Lecture Hall
http://www.utexas.edu/world/lecture/

A few colleges and universities are beginning to experiment with offering courses over the Internet. Colorado State University's Graduate School of Business <http://cobweb.cobus.colostate.edu/html/dosted/surge.nclk> offers an MBA via the World Wide Web and video-conferencing. A Web-based Master's degree in instructional and performance technology can be earned through the Graduate Instructional Performance Technology department at Boise State University <http://www-cot.idbsu.edu/~ipt/ipt_g.htm>. While most of the early entrants into Internet-based graduate curriculum have been in the fields of business or computer technologies, colleges of education are sure to follow soon. The merits of such programs will certainly be debated for some time and quality will surely vary; nevertheless it is a development worth monitoring. Particularly for educators in remote regions, this may represent a fruitful opportunity for professional development.

NEWSGROUPS

Newsgroups (sometimes referred to as USENET News) function much like public message boards on which anyone can post an article or piece of information. Most are freely accessible and readers can reply to previously posted messages. At least 17,000 newsgroups currently exist, covering virtually every conceivable topic, from abdominal training to Zoroastrianism. Most newsgroups focus on highly specialized interests, such as those related to education. Some of the newsgroups most relevant to teaching social studies are listed at the end of each content area section in this book. A good listing can be found at <http://www.dejanews.com/toplevel.html>. (Remember not to type the < >'s.)

How Do Newsgroups work?

A message "posted" to a newsgroup is automatically passed to thousands of "news servers" (archives for posted messages), usually worldwide. (Technically, network news is transferred by USENET, rather than by the Internet, but since many USENET sites are connected to the Internet, messages do make their way there.) "Newsreader" software is needed to view newsgroup messages. Browsers such as Netscape have incorporated such newsreaders and are capable of reading and replying to news. After reading a news item you may choose to respond to the topic under discussion. You can reply by e-mail to the specific individual who posted the original message, or you may post a follow-up message, which will be distributed to the entire newsgroup. A frequent error made by "newbies" is to inadvertently post their reply to the entire newsgroup while only intending to communicate with one individual. Messages for newsgroups can also be printed or saved.

Newsgroup articles get clustered in "topics." Typically, a theme is introduced when a newsgroup participant posts a question (e.g., "Are there any good films for teaching about F.D.R.'s New Deal?"). Readers will then respond with their suggestions. Some of these replies may generate further reaction from other participants. In some professional newsgroups, much valuable information and useful, creative ideas can emerge from these free-wheeling discussions. The collections of posted messages clustering around common questions or themes are called "message threads."

Newsgroups vary greatly in their style and tone. Some are very formal, with scholarly commentary, and others are informal chat. The largest are often international and read by thousands of people each day.

Most newgroups maintain archives of past messages which can provide much useful information. Fortunately, just as "search engines" can seek out Web pages containing keywords (for example, "presidential veto"), some (such as AltaVista) can also search newsgroup discussions for mention of the topics you specify. Very broad categories (e.g., "psychology") will generate thousands of hits, so it is essential to use several descriptive terms (such as "psychology lesson plans") to narrow the focus of the search.

Estimates are that the volume of information housed in the newsgroups doubles every twelve months.

Where to Begin

As mentioned earlier, a special piece of software called a "newsreader" is required to view newsgroup articles. Many browsers, such as Netscape, have internal readers, and online services, such as America Online or CompuServe, provide readers as part of their home page software. In addition, several freeware readers are available. Check the lists of newsgroups in this book for those which seem related to your interests. Many newsreaders include a query filter, allowing you to screen for only certain topics, authors, or newsgroups.

A special newsgroup exists just for "Newbies": news.announce. newusers. Check their FAQ (Frequently Asked Questions) file for information on various newsgroups and general suggestions on getting the most out of newsgroups.

Locating Newsgroups

With some 17,000 newsgroups the challenge will be deciding which are most relevant to your interests. This book offers recommendations of the most useful ones for each social studies area.

A complete list of newsgroups can be found at <http://www.de janews.com/toplevel.html>. (Remember not to type the < >'s.) Two convenient resources for locating newsgroups related to specific topic areas are Deja News at <http://www.dejanews.com/> and AltaVista <http://www.altavista.digital.com/>. When using AltaVista be sure to change the "Search" pull-down menu from "the Web" to Usenet. Enter the key word or phrase (e.g., Medieval England). A list of usegroups

Newsgroup Prefixes

Here are some of the more common prefixes representing different newsgroup categories:

alt	Alternative discussions; not carried by some sites. Quality can vary greatly as most are not moderated. Anyone could easily start an "alt" group without seeking formal approval.
bionet	Biology discussion
bit	Discussions originating from Bitnet Listserv mailing lists (a category declining in usage)
biz	Business discussions; the only categogy where posting commercial articles is permitted
comp	Computer-related topics
humanities	Literature, fine arts, and other humanities
k12	Education
misc	Miscellaneous discussions. Don't fit under any other category.
news	Discussion of network news and software used to read or transmit news articles
rec	Recreation/hobby discussions
sch	School, more education-related items
sci	Science
soc	Social issues
talk	Idle chatter
uk	Originating in the United Kingdom

where that topic has been discussed will be generated. If you are a "newbie" to newsgroups, both of the above are valuable places to start. Both provide an interface to newsgroups, letting you easily search, read, and participate.

It may be wise to simply read the posting without participating until you determine the tone of the group. Many newsgroup participants are quite satisfied to "lurk" (participate passively by only reading others' messages, but not submitting messages).

Newsgroup "Netiquette"

A number of conventions have evolved into a code of Internet etiquette, or "netiquette." Most involve common courtesies and assure that the rights of other users are not abused. Violations will often result in "flaming," or nasty messages from other users. It is wise to become familiar with "netiquette" before you begin posting messages, and to review it with your students if they have access to the Internet. Here are a few of the more common expectations:

▲ Avoid excessive use of CAPITALS or punctuation!!!! On the computer monitor, these are the equivalent of shouting.

▲ Only post messages relevant to the focus of that newsgroup. That is why it is best to "lurk" a while before entering the discussion.

▲ Don't post messages until you've read that newsgroup's FAQ (Frequently Asked Questions) file to avoid repetition. Most groups regularly post their FAQ file. Failure to check it is inviting a flame (abusive retort from other readers). For example, the FAQ file on USENET can be found on the World Wide Web at <http://www.landfield.com/faqs/>. (Note: only enter the characters between the < >'s.) A master index of FAQ files for almost all newsgroups can be accessed through the Web at <http://www.landfield. com/faqs/by-newsgroup/> or at <http://www. lib.ox.ac.uk/internet/ news/>.

▲ Remember that there may be some unstable characters participating in newsgroups. If someone should "flame" you, don't bother trying to reply. Avoid taking it personally.

▲ It is considered bad form to ask participants in a newsgroup to reply by e-mail just because you don't normally read the newsgroup. This is perceived as a tad arrogant.

▲ Generally, it is not a good idea to crosspost messages to several newsgroups. Find the one which seems most likely to attract interested readers and stick with that one.

▲ Pick a subject header which clearly describes the topic of your message. Most readers scan the headers and delete without reading those which do not immediately grab their attention.

▲ Avoid long rambling messages. If you want people to read your message, keep it concise.

▲ Be aware that commercial solicitations are severely frowned upon in most newsgroups. The general rule of thumb is to take the time to learn where your advertisement is appropriate before you post it. If you are not sure, don't post it. Another wise practice is that unless the group's charter or FAQ specifically mentions that some limited types of advertising are welcome, you should assume that no commercial postings are allowed.

▲ Any kind of chain letter will bring down the wrath of fellow users. Expect serious flaming if you violate this norm.

▲ Avoid posting personal identifying information (either your own or someone else's) on a newsgroup. Definitely do not post telephone numbers, addresses, or social security numbers.

MAILING LISTS

Similar to newsgroups, mailing lists (often called "listservs" or "discussion groups") provide a forum for discussion of common interests. The main difference is that users have to subscribe to mailing lists. Subscriptions are generally free and most mailing lists are open to the public. Some are moderated, meaning the list "owner" or sponsor screens the messages for appropriateness and relevance before posting them to the rest of the subscribers. This is not an unusual practice among more professional or academic mailing lists. The most relevant mailing lists for teaching social studies are listed at the end of each subject area section in this book.

Subscribing to Mailing Lists

Though there may occasionally be exceptions, generally it is possible to subscribe to a mailing list or discussion group by sending an e-mail message to the "LISTSERV" address with a "SUBSCRIBE" command in the message box. (Note: some use "MAJORDOMO" or "LISTPROC" instead of the LISTSERV address, but the process is essentially the same.) The addresses for subscribing to the mailing list are included with all the listings in this book.

Do not send the subscribe (or unsubscribe) request to the list itself, as that address is used only for sending messages to all the other list subscribers. The format for the subscribe command is:

Send an e-mail message to: The LISTSERV ADDRESS

Usually it is best to leave the "Subject" line blank. If your e-mail software requires something in the subject line simply type a period. The format for the message is: subscribe <List_Name> <Your_Full_Name>

For example, to subscribe to the mailing list H-AMREL on American religious history:

Send an e-mail message to: LISTSERV@H-NET.MSU.EDU

Enter the message: subscribe H-AMREL John Doe

Remember to enter your name instead of John Doe.

Additional commands may be sent to the LISTSERV (or mailing list) address.

UNSUBSCRIBE <Name of the mailing list>

LIST (to request a list of the lists at a specific site)

HELP (to receive other mailing list commands)

SET List MAIL DIGEST (to request a one-time listing of all messages, usually daily). This is a good way to check out whether a mailing list is really appropriate to your needs.

SIGNOFF <listname> to unsubscribe. (Try this if unsubscribe doesn't work.)

SET <listname> NOMAIL to stop mail temporarily.

SET <listname> MAIL to restart mail.

SET <listname> DIGEST to receive mail once a week.

MONITORING STUDENT USE OF THE INTERNET

Much attention has been focused on children's access to Web sites clearly not suited for young eyes (or old ones, in many cases). True, there are some few who choose to exploit the Internet and therefore clearly present a challenge to parents and teachers who wish to restrict student access to such adult material.

Some schools have installed filtering or blocking systems which can either block or require passwords to access the restricted sites. This is still not a guarantee that computer-literate students cannot access such sites, especially at home. Of course, you must closely monitor students to discourage use of the Internet for non-educational purposes. There are several programs that filter Internet access. Probably the three most useful in schools are: Intergo (InterGo Communications, Inc.), Specs for Kids (NewView, Inc.), and Cyber Patrol (Microsystems Software), with the last most highly recommended for its effectiveness in limiting access to adult-oriented content. It can also block outflow of information from the school's computers.

Many schools have instituted a written users' contract which students must sign before using school computers to access the Internet. The agreement specifies a code of acceptable behaviors with sanctions for their abuse.

COPYRIGHT RESTRICTIONS

Most Web sites provide direct access for sending e-mail to their Webmaster or the page's creator. It takes only a minute to send a message requesting permission to use a Web document in your classroom. Be specific, explaining exactly which items you wish to use and for what purpose. Most authors are quite pleased (and surprised) that you even ask their permission (most teachers don't), and will almost never turn down such requests. It would be wise to save any permission-granting responses in a folder on your mail server.

Many Web sites specifically grant teachers the privilege of copying content for instructional purposes. Be sure to read any "copyright" buttons which might appear on the home pages.

See any of the following resources for excellent summaries of the "fair use" guidelines:

Kenneth T. Murray (1994). Copyright and the educator. *Phi Delta Kappan*, 55, 7, 552-55.

The Untidy Issues of Copyright, Permissions, and Fair Use, and How They Affect Your Teaching,

http://www.ncte.org/news/chronicle/top/copyright.html

Copyright, Educators & Fair Use,

http://www.wstandy.com/rrweb/distresc/rrmedia/rrcpyrht.htm

Copyright: FAQs. Is the developing of course materials a "fair use"?

http://ballmer.uoregon.edu/tgleason/CopyFAQs_j385.html

While teachers do have fairly broad rights for "fair use" of copyrighted products for educational purposes, and most publishers do not actively pursue offending classroom teachers, there is an essential reason teachers should seek permission when using these materials beyond the "fair use" guidelines. Everyday teachers serve as models of morality to their students. It is a bit hypocritical to chastize students for plagarizing their papers, cheating on tests, or copying someone else's homework, if the teachers themselves then illegally use someone else's creative materials. The end really does not justify the means. With the ability to quickly send e-mail messages to the author, there really is no excuse for not seeking appropriate permission when course use exceeds "fair use" guidelines. The most important reason for doing so is: "It's the right thing to do."

Section **2**

GENERAL SOCIAL STUDIES RESOURCES

BEST WEB SITES: SOCIAL STUDIES

Comment	### Arts & Entertainment Television
	http://www.aetv.com/aeclassroom/index.html
	This listing of upcoming educational programs is filled with valuable social studies lessons for classroom teachers. All are materials related to A&E cable channel programming. These excellent lesson plans would have the greatest value when used with the accompanying broadcast, but would be useful even if the program is not available. Teachers are permitted to copy the commercial-free programs for classroom use. Copies of previous programs are available for purchase at a very reasonable cost. A small sampling of recent programs:
	Susan B. Anthony: Rebel for the Cause—Thursday Eleanor Roosevelt: A Restless Spirit— Thursday Alexander Graham Bell: Voice of Invention The American Revolution: The Conflict Ignites The Hindenberg—Monday Stalin: Red Terror The Power and the Drama of Leadership
	[A&E Television Networks]
Comment	### Classroom Connect
	http://www.classroom.net/
	This award-winning commercial site is designed to promote its newsletter subscriptions. However, a reasonable assortment of free items is also available. Links are provided to K-12 educational resources on the Internet. An interactive database for exchanging teaching ideas with other teachers and regularly scheduled online discussions on selected topics should both be of value to social studies teachers.
	[Classroom Connect]
Comment	### CMARGIN
	http://www.cmargin.com/notes.html
	Each weekday, this free e-mail service provides K-12 teachers with worthwhile items gleaned from newspapers and other publications. The emphasis is upon helping students see the real-world relevance of what they are studying. As a commercial enterprise, advertisements are prominently dis-

played, but not overbearing. Items are presented in the following ten categories:

Real-World Math
Real-World Science
Real-World Literacy
Historical Perspective
Economic Perspective
Geographic Perspective
Civic Perspective
Education in the News
Kids in the News
Fun Facts and Real-World Data

[Margin Media Ventures]

Computers in the Social Studies

Comment

http://www.cssjournal.com/journal/

Social studies teachers with an interest in using computers as part of their curriculum should find this journal of great value. Various practical articles appear in each issue. A copy of the current issue may be viewed online; however, only subscribers may access the archive of past issues. Published six times a year, the cost is a reasonable $10.00 for individuals for a two-year subscription and $20.00 for institutions per yearly subscription. (It's pretty common practice to have a higher institutional rate.) Subscription forms may be obtained online.

[CSS Journal]

A+

ERIC Clearinghouse for Social Studies/ Social Science Education ERIC/ChESS

Comment

http://www.indiana.edu/~ssdc/eric-chess.html

ERIC/ChESS, a nationwide depository of current social studies education materials, holds curriculum guides, journal articles, teaching units, research reports, and bibliographies. Its most useful feature is probably the "AskERIC" function, which permits teachers to tap the vast ERIC database by submitting e-mail questions or to conduct online keyword searches. Abstracts of ERIC documents are available, but the complete item must be purchased or viewed at a library which has the microfiche document. A small selection of lesson plans is available.

[Social Studies Development Center of Indiana University, U.S. Department of Education]

Comment

History/Social Studies Web Site for K-12 Teachers

http://www.execpc.com/~dboals/boals.html

This site contains hundreds of links to Web sites related to teaching history and social studies, though only some are annotated. The quality of the individual sites varies greatly. Worth browsing if you are not in a hurry.

[Dennis Boals]

Comment

INFOMINE K-12 Education & Instructional Resource Facilitator

_A+_

http://lib-www.ucr.edu/k12info.html

Thousands of resources for teaching just about any topic included in K-12 education will be found through this powerful organizational tool. The massive amount of information listed and the lack of a systematic rating system sometimes make this an overwhelming resource. If you have the time, many gems can be found hidden among this massive collection of Web sites.

[Regents of the University of California]

Comment

Lesson Plans and Resources for Social Studies Teachers

http://www.csun.edu/~hcedu013/index.html

This lesson archive houses a colorful, complete collection of lesson plans, teaching strategies and online activities. An excellent listing of newsgroups and mailing lists of interest to social studies teachers is also included. Well worth a look.

[Marty Levine, California State University, Northridge]

Comment

National Council for History Education

http://www.history.inter.net/nche/

Intended as an advocate and supportive resource for all who teach history, from kindergarten to doctoral students, the N.C.H.E. provides a number of helpful services and publications. Professional development opportunities, new books and other teaching media, links to history-related Web sites, and membership information are available through its home page. Current and archived issues of its online monthly newsletter _History Matters!_ provide ideas, notes, and news about teaching history.

[National Council for History Education]

Comment	**National Council for the Social Studies** http://www.ncss.org/online// This is the home page of the largest national association promoting the teaching of social studies. This site is useful for locating instructional resources for teaching social studies, though most must be purchased either from outside vendors or the N.C.S.S. A limited number of lesson plans from the N.C.S.S. journal, *Social Education*, can be downloaded. The N.C.S.S. Online Conference Room hosts discussions among educators. A Java-compatible browser such as Netscape 3.0 is required to access the chat line. [National Council for the Social Studies]
Comment	**NickNacks: Telecollaborate** http://www1.minn.net:80/~schubert/NickNacks.html Join the global classroom by collaborating on Internet learning projects. Propose your own project or join in those started by teachers and students around the world. A good place to browse for ideas. [Nancy Schubert]
Comment	**Teacher Talk** http://education.indiana.edu/cas/tt/tthmpg.html Written for beginning secondary teachers, this online magazine offers many sound, practical tips for handling the daily challenges of classroom teaching. Themes covered so far include mental health, sex issues in the classroom, community building, classroom management, cultural diversity, violence in the schools, student teaching, and teen use of alcohol. A few ideas for lesson plans are also included in each issue. [Center for Adolescent Studies, Indiana University]
Comment	**Teachers Helping Teachers** http://www.pacificnet.net/~mandel/ Teachers offer help to their colleagues through this online idea exchange. A special section on teaching social studies and another on classroom management should be of interest. [Scott Mandel]

ELECTRONIC MAILING LISTS: SOCIAL STUDIES

Many electronic mailing lists focus on topics of interest to social studies teachers, and it is easy to subscribe. For example, to subscribe to the mailing list AEELIST of the Association for Experimental Education:

Send an e-mail message to: LISTSERV@PUCC.PRINCETON.EDU

Usually it is best to leave the "Subject" line blank. If your e-mail software requires something in the subject line, simply type a period. Enter the message: subscribe AEELIST John Doe. The format for the message is: subscribe <List_Name> <Your_Full_Name>.

Here is a selection of mailing lists of interest to many teachers. Those focusing upon a specific subject area (such as world history or sociology) will be found under the various social studies subjects later in this book. The ones listed below are more general in their focus.

AEELIST

Association for Experimental Education

E-mail to: LISTSERV@PUCC.PRINCETON.EDU

AERA

The American Educational Research Association sponsors a variety of sublists on the following topics:

AERA-GSL	Graduate Studies List
AERA-A	Educational Administration Forum
AERA-B	Curriculum Studies Forum
AERA-C	Learning and Instruction
AERA-D	Measurement and Research Methodology
AERA-E	Counseling and Human Development
AERA-F	History and Historiography
AERA-G	Social Context of Education
AERA-H	School Evaluation and Program Development
AERA-I	Education in the Professions
AERA-J	Postsecondary Education
AERA-K	Teaching and Teacher Education

E-mail to: LISTSERV@ASU.EDU

On the message line enter the name of the subgroup desired.

Altlearn

Alternative approaches to learning

E-mail to: LISTSERV@SJUVM.STJOHNS.EDU

ASAT-EVA

Distance learning forum

E-mail to: LISTSERV@UNLVM.UNL.EDU

C-Edres
Source for educational resources on the Internet
E-mail to: C-EDRES-SERVER@UNB.CA

DCS-Lite
Provides teachers with weekly announcements of copyright-cleared Discovery Channel programs. No discussion on this list.
E-mail to: LISTSERV@LISTS.DISCOVERY.COM

Discovery-School
Informs teachers of upcoming copyright-cleared Discovery Channel programs. Forum to exchange ideas about using Discovery Channel programming in the classroom.
E-mail to: LISTSERV@LISTS.DISCOVERY.COM

Ednet
Discussion of issues related to educational networks
E-mail to: LISTSERV@LISTS.UMASS.EDU

Edstyle
Forum on educational learning styles
E-mail to: LISTSERV@SJUVM.STJOHNS.EDU

Edtech
Educational technology issues
E-mail to: LISTSERV@MSU.EDU

Education-Consumers
General discussion of school reform and criticism
E-mail to: MAJORDOMO@XTN.NET

Effschprac
Effective schools practices forum
E-mail to: MAILSERV@OREGON.UOREGON.EDU

Ekids
Electronic Kids
E-mail to: MAJORDOMO@CITYBEACH.WA.EDU.AU

Eled-L
Elementary education concerns and ideas
E-mail to: LISTSERV@KSUVM.KSU.EDU

IECC
Teachers seeking worldwide "Key-Pal" exchanges
E-mail to: REQUEST@STOLAF.EDU

IECC-Discussion
Discussions about cross-cultural communications and educational uses of e-mail
E-mail to: IECC-DiscussioN-REQUEST@STOLAF.EDU

IECC-Projects
Teachers desiring to establish e-mail exchanges or cross-cultural projects
E-mail to: IECC-PROJECTS-REQUEST@STOLAF.EDU

Inclass
Ideas on using the Internet in the classroom
E-mail to: LISTPROC@SCHOOLNET.CARLETON.CA

Infolist
Discussion of Internet resources
E-mail to: MAJORDOMO@GSN.ORG

Inter-L
Use of the Internet in education
E-mail to: LISTPROC2@BGU.EDU

Kidcafe
Discussion group for young students
E-mail to: LISTSERV@VM1.NODAK.EDU

Kidintro
Pen pal group for children
E-mail to: LISTSERV@SJUVM.STJOHNS.EDU

Kids-Act
Activities and project ideas for kids
E-mail to: LISTSERV@VM1.NODAK.EDU

Kidsphere
International Kidslink discussion group
E-mail to: KIDSPHERE@VMS.CIS.PITT.EDU

L-Aclrng
Active and collaborative learning forum
E-mail to: LISTSERV@PSUVM.PSU.EDU

Lrn-Ed
Teachers support and information
E-mail to: LISTSERV@SUVM.SYR.EDU

Middle-L
Discussion for junior high/middle school-age students
E-mail to: LISTSERV@VMD.CSO.UIUC.EDU

Mult-Ed
Multicultural education
E-mail to: LISTPROC@GMU.EDU

Multc-Ed
Multicultural education list
E-mail to: LISTSERV@UMDD.UMD.EDU

Multicultural-Ed
Another forum for multicultural education discussions
E-mail to: LISTPROC@LISTS.FSU.EDU

Network-Nuggets-L
Useful educational resources to be found on the Internet
E-mail to: LISTPROC@CLN.ETC.BC.CA

Penpal-L
Electronic pen pals can be linked here
E-mail to: LISTSERV@UNCCVM.UNCC.EDU

School-L
K-12 education discussion
E-mail to: LISTSERV@IRLEARN.UCD.IE

Sigtel-L
Telecommunications in education
E-mail to: LISTPROC@LIST.ACS.OHIO-STATE.EDU

Superk12
Tapping the Information Superhighway as an instructional tool
E-mail to: LISTSERV@SUVM.SYR.EDU

Tag-L
Talented and gifted education
E-mail to: LISTSERV@LISTSERV.NODAK.EDU

Teacheft
Teaching effectiveness forum
E-mail to: LISTSERV@WCUPA.EDU

WWWEDU
Use of the World Wide Web in education
E-mail to: LISTPROC@READY.CPB.ORG

Education Newsgroups

k12.chat.elementary	Assorted topics of interest to elementary kids
k12.chat.junior	Junior high/middle school chat
k12.chat.senior	General topics of interest to secondary students
k12.chat.teacher	A forum for teachers to exchange thoughts on teaching
k12.ed.life-skills	Ideas for teaching basic life skills
k12.ed.special	Special education issues
k12.ed.soc-studies	K-12 social studies education and curriculum
k12.ed.tag	Teaching talented and gifted students
k12.news	Miscellaneous items of interest to educators
misc.education	General discussion of educational issues
schl.kids.kidcafe	Largely a pen pal exchange for young students
schl.sig.k12admin	Special interest group for administrators

AMERICAN HISTORY

BEST WEB SITES: AMERICAN HISTORY

Comment	**100 Years of Radio** http://www.alpcom.it/hamradio/evitto.html In an age of cellular phones, telecommunications satellites, and color television, it is difficult to imagine a time when radios did not exist. Yet only 100 years ago, radio was but a dream in the creative mind of Guglielmo Marconi. This information-packed Web page showcases the evolution of radio. [Andrea Borgnino, Angelo Brunero, and CSP Staff]
Comment	**1492: An Ongoing Voyage** http://lcweb.loc.gov/exhibits/1492/intro.html Though not the first white man to "discover" the new world, Christopher Columbus' historic voyages certainly affected the development of both Europe and the American continent. This Library of Congress online exhibit considers the causes and effects of his venture in six outstanding displays: What Came To Be Called "America" The Mediterranean World Christopher Columbus: Man and Myth Inventing America Europe Claims America Epilogue [Library of Congress]
Comment	**A Nation Divided** http://www.historyplace.com/civilwar/index.html This bookstore-sponsored Web site features a Civil War timeline including related quotations and photographs. The great selection of old photographs makes a visit worthwhile. [The History Place]
Comment	**Abraham Lincoln Online** http://www.netins.net/showcase/creative/lincoln.html Representing the best of online history-related resources, this is an excellent site, devoted exclusively to our 16th president. The section on Lincoln's Thinking provides intriguing insights into his thought processes. Many fascinating discussions, often

A+

by Lincoln scholars, can be tapped in the Lincoln Mailbag. Contents are well-organized in the following categories:

> Lincoln This Week
> Monthly Quiz
> Speeches/Writings
> Historic Sites
> Lincoln Resources
> Lincoln's Thinking
> News and Events
> Lincoln Mailbag
> Index to Links
> Lincoln Book Talk
> Lincoln Bookshelf

[Rhoda Sneller]

African-American Mosaic

Comment

http://lcweb.loc.gov/exhibits/african/intro.html

This "Resource Guide for the Study of Black History and Culture" provides a sampler of the African-American collection housed in the Library of Congress. The collection includes books, photographs, film, music, periodicals, prints, and recordings, covering almost 500 years of the black experience in the Western hemisphere. The exhibit contains items from four areas: Colonization, Abolition, Migrations, and the WPA. The Library of Congress deserves praise for making a portion of its vast resources accessible to the entire world via Cyberspace technology. Hopefully, many more projects of this caliber will follow.

[Library of Congress]

African-American History

Comment

http://detnews.com/blkhist/9602/05/intro/intro.html

What was the connection between the Exodusters of 1879 and desegregation of American schools in the 1960s and '70s? The answer to this and many other questions about the history of African Americans is included in this online quiz.

[The Detroit News]

Alexander Graham Bell's Path to the Telephone

Comment

http://jefferson.village.virginia.edu/albell/homepage.html

The invention of the telephone was not a single event but the product of many ideas, experiments, and innovations by Bell and many others. This scholarly, text-heavy resource provides a detailed account of the scientific process followed by Bell in creating his telephone. Links to online versions of Alexander Graham Bell's notebooks are worth exploring.

[Michael E. Gorman, Technology, Culture & Communications, University of Virginia]

Age of Imperialism

Comment

http://www.smplanet.com/imperialism/teacher.html

"The Age of Imperialism" is a chapter from *An On-line History of the United States*, an interactive teaching tool utilizing the array of Internet resources. This well-written, engaging unit enhances students' understanding of the nineteenth-century foreign policy known as expansionism or imperialism, and the motivation behind the United States' adoption of this policy. Effective use of maps, photographs, and other primary documents enriches the value of these lessons and stimulate student interest.

[Small Planet Communications, Inc.]

American Civil War

Comment

http://ananke.advanced.org/3055/netscape/index.html

Check the "Fun Fact of the Day" for interest-arousing tidbits to display as posters or overheads.

[Chris Johnson, Joe Simonson, or Dale Webster]

American Civil War Home Page

A+

Comment

http://funnelweb.utcc.utk.edu/~hoemann/warweb.html

Outstanding collection of dozens of hypertext links to the most valuable electronic resources about the American Civil War (1861-1865). Small sampling of links:

> Graphic Images
> Letters, Accounts, Diaries and Other Documentary Records
> A Civil War Chronology
> The Gettysburg Archive
> National Museum of Civil War Medicine
> Rosters of Combatants

[George H. Hoemann and Mary E. Myers]

American Civil War Information Archive

Comment

http://www.access.digex.net/~bdboyle/cw.html

A poignant letter written by a grieving mother to her soldier-son telling him of his brother's death is but one gem hidden within this gold mine of Civil War resources. This award-winning site is a rich depository of potentially useful teaching material. Dozens of links, and some items probably found nowhere else on the Web, make this an essential stop for Civil War buffs and history teachers. Be sure to check out the alt.war.civil.usa newsgroup archive which is stored here. The Trivia Tests could be adapted as interest-grabbing class activities.

[Bryan D. Boyle]

The American Experience

Comment

http://www.pbs.org/wgbh/pages/amex/aeabout.html

Since 1988, PBS has broadcast *The American Experience*, a splendid, award-winning, historical documentary series produced by WBGH. The series has featured outstanding biographies of the noble and notorious, gripping stories of natural disasters, the tragedies of wartime, and the challenges faced by a diverse population. News of upcoming productions can be found on this Web page. Teacher guides are available for some programs. Videotapes of previously aired programs can be inexpensively (often less than $20 per tape) purchased through WBGH.

[WBGH; Public Broadcasting System]

American History Archive Project

Comment

http://www.ilt.columbia.edu/k12/history/aha.html

This well-organized archive of Web links to American history resources includes interesting samples of student Web page history projects. These can serve as useful models for motivating Web-wise classes.

[Institute for Learning Technologies]

American History: The History Net Archives

Comment

http://www.thehistorynet.com/THNarchives/
AmericanHistory/

Every history teacher should bookmark this megasite, over-flowing with excellent content, superbly written articles, and beautiful color images. Unlike most archives, which are merely collections of links to other sites, the History Net contains a large archive of original items. Truly an exemplary site. Just a small sample of the articles contained in the archives:

> 1797: The First Real Election
> Blue Ridge Traditions
> Civil War Railroads
> The Death and Life of Stonewall Jackson
> Horsepower Moves the Guns
> Life in Early America: The Worst Winters
> Little Bighorn Coverup
> The Negro Leagues: How Good Were They?
> Personality: Henry Ford
> Undercover: German Saboteurs in America

[American Historical Society]

American Immigration

Comment

http://www.bergen.org/AAST/Projects/Immigration/

Though constructed by two tenth-grade history students, this imaginative Web page offers a serious look at immigration to America from 1607 to the present. Various sections examine why people immigrated, who came, where they settled, how they traveled, how they were treated, and the impact they had on America. Thought-provoking quotations about immigration are also featured.

[Jonathan Lee and Robert Siemborski]

A+

American Life Histories

Comment

http://lcweb2.loc.gov/ammem/wpaintro/wpalife.html

Collected from 1936 to 1940 as part of the Folklore Project and the Federal Writers' Project for the U.S. Works Progress Administration (WPA), some 2,900 documents provide a glimpse of the life and work of men and women from various occupations, ethnic backgrounds, and geographical regions. For $20 a week unemployed writers recorded the life histories of 10,000 women and men, such as a Vermont farm wife, a Scandinavian iron worker, a clerk in Macy's department store, a Texas dynamiter, a Georgia washwoman, or a Vermont granite carver. The fascinating histories describe the individual's job, lifestyle, income, political views, religion and values, physical and medical condition, and diet. Most of the interviewees had been born before 1900, and many relayed firsthand accounts of memorable events in their lives, such as meeting Billy the Kid, making the pioneer journey west by covered wagon, or surviving the Chicago fire of 1871. The interviews can be searched by keyword or browsed by state. This vast treasure, until recently almost forgotten in the Library of Congress archives, provides a virtual gateway to the past.

[Library of Congress]

A+

American Memory Collection

Comment

http://lcweb2.loc.gov/ammem/amtitle.new.html

The Library of Congress serves as the collective American memory. The library has constructed several exceptional online exhibits from its special collections. Constructed of primary resources and archival items, the exhibit contains prints and photographs, text documents, motion pictures, and sound recordings. Pathfinder indexes help users navigate the American Memory historical collections and keyword searches facilitate quick location of materials related to a specific interest. Each of the twenty exhibits merits a look. More are planned for the future, so check back frequently. Current exhibits:

African-American Perspectives
Selected Civil War Photographs
Evolution of the Conservation Movement, 1850-1920
Continental Congress and the Constitutional Convention
America's First Look into the Camera: Daguerreotype Portraits and Views, 1842-1862
Touring Turn-of-the-Century America: Photographs from the Detroit Publishing Company 1880-1920
Color Photographs from the Farm Security Administration and the Office of War Information 1938-1944
American Life Histories: Manuscripts from the Federal Writers' Project, 1936-1940
Early Motion Pictures, 1897-1916
Creative Americans: Portraits by Carl Van Vechten, 1932-1964
Portraits of the Presidents and First Ladies, 1789-Present
America's Leaders Speak: Recordings from World War I and the 1920 Election
The American Variety Stage: Vaudeville and Popular Entertainment, 1870-1920
Votes for Women: Selections from the National American

Woman Suffrage Association Collection, 1848-1921
Recovered Notebooks from the Thomas Biggs Harned Walt
Whitman Collection
Washington as It Was: Photographs by Theodor Horydczak,
1923-1959
Around the World in the 1890s: Photographs from the
World's Transportation Commission, 1894-1896
Built in America: Historic American Buildings
Survey/Historic American Engineering Record, 1933-Present
Presidential Papers

[Library of Congress; National Digital Library]

American Prohibition

Comment

http://www.cohums.ohio-state.edu/history/projects/
prohibition/def ault.htm

A link-reliant, though interesting, view of American prohibition in the 1920s. Hypertext links to documents such as George Kibbe Turner's 1907 McClure's Magazine article on "The City of Chicago, A Study of the Great Immoralities" enrich one's understanding of this complex era.

[K. Austin Kerr, Department of History, Ohio State University]

American Revolutionary War Web Site

Comment

http://www.ccs.neu.edu/home/bcortez/revwar/revwar.html

Designed by and for Revolutionary War re-enactors, the "RevWeb" lists both American Colonial and British Empire re-enactor units throughout the United States. Excellent field trips can be arranged to visit local engagements or invite local re-enactors to visit your classes in authentic regalia.

[B. Cortez, Northwestern University]

Anonymous Account of the Boston Massacre

Comment

http://grid.let.rug.nl/~welling/usa/documents/bostanon.html

In 1849, this eyewitness account of the famed Boston Massacre was published. It is reprinted here with hypertext links to related articles.

[Dep. Alfa, Informatica, University of Groningen]

Anacostia Museum

http://www.si.edu/organiza/museums/anacost/welcome.htm

A small collection of exhibits focuses on the historical black experience in Washington, D.C., and the rural South. A brief description of each of the following exhibits and accompanying photographs are included:

Black Mosaic: Community, Race, and Ethnicity among Black Immigrants in Washington, D.C.
Climbing Jacob's Ladder: The Rise of Black Churches in Eastern American Cities, 1740-1877
The Real McCoy, African American Invention and Innovation, 1619-1930
The Renaissance: Black Arts of the Twenties
The Meaning of Kwanzaa

[The Smithsonian Institution]

Anti-Imperialism in the United States (1898-1935)

http://www.rochester.ican.net/~fjzwick/ail98-35.html

Organized opposition to the United States' territorial expansionist policy of imperialism first arose during the Spanish-American War. Students are encouraged to critically examine this issue through a set of carefully selected primary resources: anti-imperialist literature, newspaper and magazine articles, political cartoons, speeches, and pamphlets. Be sure to read the Citation and Permissions Guide for information on using the resources from this site for classroom use.

[Jim Zwick, Syracuse University]

Archiving Early America

http://earlyamerica.com/

Tap this well-designed electronic time capsule to bring history of eighteenth-century America to life by building lessons around primary source materials: colorful maps, original newspapers, and writings, such as Ben Franklin's autobiography. Have students read the classified ads of the January 2, 1750 issue of *The Pennsylvania Gazette* to draw conclusions about the needs, wants, values, and culture of these early Americans. The unique article, "How To Read A 200-Year-Old Document," should prove helpful in teaching students to use original documents. A partial listing of original eighteenth-century "Milestone Historic Documents" is available in this virtual archive:

> The Treaty of Greenville
> Thomas Paine's "Common Sense"
> The Articles of Confederation
> George Washington's Journal
> The Declaration of Arms
> The Paris Peace Treaty of 1783
> Declaration of Rights
> Jay's Treaty
> The Northwest Ordinance
> First State of the Union Address

[Don Vitale]

Ask Thomas Jefferson

Comment

http://www.mit.edu:8001/activities/libertarians/
ask-thomas-jefferson/jefferson.html

Quotations from Thomas Jefferson are used to answer questions about politics, history, religion, literature, human nature, and society.

His view on federal debt?

"I place economy among the first and important virtues, and public debt as the greatest of dangers. To preserve our independence, we must not let our rulers load us with perpetual debt. We must make our choice between economy and liberty, or profusion and servitude. If we can prevent the government from wasting the labours of the people under the pretense of caring for them, they will be happy."

—Thomas Jefferson

[MIT Libertarian Club]

Benjamin Franklin: Glimpses of the Man

Comment

http://sln.fi.edu/franklin/rotten.html

An impressive multimedia site is dedicated to one of eighteenth-century America's most talented individuals. The feats of arguably the most versatile character in American history are detailed in hypertext links through this biographical site. Many of his achievements as inventor, scientist, printer, statesman, musician, philosopher, and economist are highlighted, though his scientific contributions receive greatest attention.

[The Franklin Institute Science Museum]

Comment	**Black History** http://www.kn.pacbell.com/wired/BHM/AfroAm.html Find a dozen teaching activities for teaching issues related to African-American history. The lessons cover such topics as slavery, African-American leaders, institutional changes, and Black History Month. [Pacific Bell]
Comment	**Civil War Letters Home** http://www.ucsc.edu/civil-war-letters/home.html Letters written by Newton Robert Scott, Private, Company A, of the 36th Infantry, Iowa Volunteers are included in this fascinating archive. Most of Scott's letters were written to Hannah Cone, a neighbor in Albia, Iowa. The last letter was written to his parents just before he was mustered out in August of 1865. Scott's letters to Hannah give a detailed glimpse of daily life in the Union Army camps. The disappointment of the soldiers in the handling of the war by Washington politicians was evident in his writings. Newton and Hannah later married and had nine children. These beautiful letters must truly be treasured by his descendants. [William Scott Proudfoot]
Comment	**Civil War Slang** http://www.direclynx.net/~russward/223/slang.html A list of words and phrases which originated during the U.S. Civil War are included in this archive. Samples include: Arkansas toothpick (large knife) bread basket (stomach) chief cook and bottle washer (person capable of doing many things) fit to be tied (angry) greenbacks (money) horse sense (smart, on the ball) hunkey dorey (great!) pepperbox (pistol) [223rd Signal Corps]
Comment	**Civil War Letters of a Jewish Soldier** http://www.access.digex.net/~bdboyle/jewish.html

A young Jewish man writes of the challenges and daily events of a Civil War soldier. In one letter he describes the care of the wounded in make-shift hospitals, and on the tireless work of Dorothea Dix, who served as Superintendent of Women Nurses for the Union.

Civil War Letters of J. C. Cohen

Comment

http://www.access.digex.net/~bdboyle/cohen.html

J. C. Cohen served with the 27th Ohio Infantry, known as the "Army of the Mississippi." The full text of seven articles and a set of poems sent back to *The Jewish Messenger* chronicle his experiences in Mississippi and Tennessee.

"It seems to be pretty clearly demonstrated that the Army of the Tennessee wants a leader; that is, a man who is free from the prevalent disease of Canal on the brain; a man who can refrain from kicking Israelites out of his back door, while the enemy enter at the front; a man who is a man, and a General; one who is free from the bigoted principles which are demoralizing our army and rendering our success more uncertain and distant."
—J.C.Cohen
  Corinth, Miss., May 6th, 1863

[Bryan Boyle's Bronx Bulletin Board]

Civil War Resources

Comment

http://www.vmi.edu/~archtml/cwsource.html

Civil War era artifacts and documents from the VMI Archives are included in this superb collection. Special collections focus on the death of Stonewall Jackson and the Battle of New Market. The vivid first-person accounts enrich the textbook descriptions of battles and numbers of casualties. Full text manuscripts written by Virginian participants in the Civil War include the following:

> William J. Black Diary. Shoemaker's Co., Virginia Horse Artillery
> Henry H. Dedrick Papers. Private, 52nd Virginia Infantry
> Stonewall Jackson Papers. Pre-war VMI Faculty; CSA General
> Matthew Fontaine Maury Papers. Naval officer; oceanographer; Confederate Navy; post-war VMI faculty
> New Market Collection. Memoirs of battle veterans

[Virginia Military Institute Archives]

Comment	**Consider the Source**
	
	http://www.sara.nysed.gov/services/teachers/ctspromo.htm
	
	The Forward, Table of Contents, and three lesson plans from *Consider the Source: Historical Records in the Classroom* are featured online. The 146-page book was published by the New York State Archives and Records Administration to help teachers develop lesson plans incorporating primary resources. Information on purchasing the book ($10) can be found on the home page. The online lessons include:
	
	    1825 Erie Canal Broadside
	    The 1903 Survey of Industrial Discharges and Sewage
	    The Vietnam-Era Documents
	
	[New York State Archives and Records Administration]

Comment	**Constitutional Issues: Separation of Powers** http://www.nara.gov/nara/digital/teaching/conissues/separat.html The principle of separation of powers within the United States government was seriously challenged in 1937, when Franklin Roosevelt proposed to increase the number of Justices on the Supreme Court. Employing online copies of a primary document from the National Archives, teachers can lead students through a discussion and activities examining the causes and effects of Roosevelt's scheme. [National Archives and Records Administration]
Comment	**Daguerreotypes** http://www.austinc.edu/dag View or download images of stunning nineteenth-century daguerreotypes from a large gallery. The site also includes a short history of the daguerreotype and an illustrated depiction of the process. Must have graphic capability to enjoy the beauty of these images. Though the images are copyrighted, use for classroom instruction is permitted. [The Daguerreian Society]
Comment	**Declarations of the Causes of Secession** http://www.access.digex.net/~bdboyle/declar.html

Declarations of Secession from the union are included for the states of Georgia, Mississippi, South Carolina, and Texas.

[Copied by Justin Sanders from J. A. May & J. R. Faunt, South Carolina Secedes, University of South Carolina Press, 1960]

Declaring Independence: Drafting the Documents

Comment

http://lcweb.loc.gov/exhibits/declara/declara1.html

A transcript of Thomas Jefferson's original rough draft of the Declaration of Independence and an 1826 letter declining to attend the fiftieth anniversary celebration of the Declaration are among the documents included in this fascinating electronic exhibit.

[Library of Congress; Xerox Foundation]

Declassified Intelligence Satellite Photographs

Comment

http://edcwww.cr.usgs.gov/dclass/dclass.html

In 1995, President Clinton issued an executive order authorizing the declassification of satellite photographs collected by U.S. intelligence during the 1960s. Specific areas can be selected or users may browse an online catalog of declassified images such as Soviet airfields, strategic bomber bases, volcanoes, and other geographic features. Eventually, over 18,000 declassified rolls of film will be available. The images suggest the immensity of the resources invested in the Cold War confrontation by both sides.

[United States Geological Survey]

Daily Almanacs

Comment

http://shoga.wwa.com/~mjm/almanac2.html

Daily postings of the anniversaries of noted historical events can be used as bulletin board displays.

[Michael J Maggio]

Diaries from the Civil War

Comment

http://jefferson.village.virginia.edu/vshadow/diary.html

Several first-person accounts from Civil War participants can be accessed here. An excerpt from the diary of Civil War soldier Samuel Cormany reads, "Our Boys opened 54 guns at the same time on the Rebel lines and works from a little conical hill, Cemetery Ridge. We were picketing in the rear and on the right of it—Many shells came our way—some really quite near—But it is wonderful how few really made our acquaintance." Diary entries detailing everyday life during the Civil War provide fascinating insights into the lives of those experiencing the war firsthand.

[Edward L. Ayers]

Donner Online

Comment

http://www.kn.pacbell.com/wired/donner/#task

This fantastic online cooperative learning activity uses the content of the Donner Party tragedy on the Oregon Trail to teach the skills of historical research and collaborative critical thinking. Students assume assigned roles (historian, diarist, cartographer, pictorialist, correspondent, provisioner, jester, or scientist) to help their team collect and analyze information. A first-rate learning activity!

[Pacific Bell]

Early American Review

Comment

http://earlyamerica.com/review/

This quarterly electronic journal chronicles the people, issues and events of eighteenth-century America. Very professionally done graphics and layout, along with splendid content, make this a site worth visiting.

[DEV Communications, Inc.]

Ellis Island Oral History Project

Comment

http://www.i-channel.com/ellis/oralhist.html

Listen to Charles Beller, who came from Russia in 1910 at the age of six as he described his journey to America and arrival and processing at the Ellis Island facility. Over 1,300 audio-taped interviews preserve the firsthand recollections of a sample of the 12 million immigrants arriving at Ellis Island between 1892 and 1954. Additional pages describe the Ellis Island Museum today and the challenges facing immigrants arriving in America in the late nineteenth and early twentieth centuries.

[The International Channel, Ellis Island Immigration Museum, National Park Service]

	Early American Review: A Journal of People, Issues, and Events in 18th Century America
Comment	http://earlyamerica.com/review/winter96/index.html
	This superb quarterly magazine features scholarly articles with vivid illustrations on a variety of topics related to this era of the American experiment. A crossword puzzle for students of history appears in each edition. Articles from past issues:
	Sons of Liberty: Patriots or Terrorists? Ticonderoga at Sunset Slavery's Roots In Early America Jefferson, Education and The Franchise Phillis Wheatley—America's First Black Poet
	[DEV Communications]
	Era of William McKinley
Comment	http://www.cohums.ohio-state.edu/history/projects/McKinley/
	A serious historical time capsule of the presidency and era of William McKinley. Coverage of Spanish-American War of 1898 and a set of political cartoons featuring William McKinley are noteworthy highlights of this attractively designed Web site. Check the link to the Anti-Saloon League.
	[Department of History, Ohio State University]
	Exploring the West from Monticello
Comment	http://www.lib.virginia.edu/exhibits/lewis_clark/home.html
	The story of Lewis and Clark's exploration of the west is detailed in a digitized version of the library exhibition created by the university founded by Thomas Jefferson. Historic maps from the time of Columbus illustrate the scholarly account of the historic adventure.
	[University of Virginia Library]
	FDR Cartoon Archive
Comment	http://www.wizvax.net/nisk_hs/departments/social/fdr_html/FDRmain.html
	The collaborative effort of a high school computer math class and a history class created this magnificant archive of cartoons about the presidency of Franklin D. Roosevelt. A

teacher's guide provides links to lesson ideas for using political cartoons which were obtained from the FDR Hyde Park Library, are arranged by subject, and can be searched using a variety of criteria. Topic headings include:

> Waiting for the New Deal
> Foreign Relations
> The First One Hundred Days
> Farm Issues
> Alphabet Soup
> Supreme Court Reform
> Labor
> The War Years

[Niskayuna High School, Niskayuna, NY]

From Revolution to Reconstruction

Comment

http://grid.let.rug.nl/%7Ewelling/usa/

Interestingly, this "HTML-hypertext on American History, from the Colonial Period until Modern Times" originates in the Netherlands. Nonetheless, it provides a superb set of links to original documents covering the span from the American Revolution to the beginning of World War I. Using the American Information Agency's booklet, "An Outline of American History," as the basic hypertext document, its links embellish the account of this period in American history.

[Arts faculty and students, University of Groningen in the Netherlands]

Great Chicago Fire

Comment

http://www.chicagohs.org/fire/intro/

The story of one of the most famous disasters in American history, the Great Chicago Fire of 1871, is told through this electronic memorial. Essays and graphic images chronologically depict the events of the fire. A second exhibit, The Web of Memory, features eyewitness accounts, poetry, assorted artifacts, contemporary news accounts, and illustrations.

[Chicago Historical Society and Academic Technologies of Northwestern University]

Great Kiva

Comment

http://www.sscf.ucsb.edu/anth/projects/great.kiva/

Several interactive, audio-visual options lead users through a virtual tour of an Anasazi prehistoric kiva. The 3-D model developed for this project is an impressive artistic achievement. The meticulous attention to detail, resplendent graphics, and scholarly accuracy mark this as one of the finest educational sites available on the World Wide Web.

[John Kantner]

Harlem Renaissance

Comment

http://encarta.msn.com/schoolhouse/harlem/harlem.asp

Marvelous coverage of the 1920s cultural movement which became known as the "Harlem Renaissance." This spurt of creative activity among black Americans influenced literature, music, and art, celebrating the uniqueness of African-American culture. In addition to biographical information on major artists and writers of the era, a lesson plan for classroom use is available.

[Encarta Schoolhouse]

Historic, Social, Economic, and Demographic Data

Comment

http://icg.harvard.edu/census/

What percent of the adults in Ohio could not read in 1850? This site could provide that answer, along with responses to thousands of other questions about the population during the formative years of the United States. Drawing from the massive federal census database compiled every ten years, a statistical overview of the United States from 1790 to 1860 provides data in the following categories:

Total Population Counts
White Population
Free Colored Population
Slave Population
Miscellaneous Population Characteristics
Education and Literacy
Mortality, Natality, and Marriage
Occupations and Economy
Churches

Dozens of statistics are available within each of these categories for analysis by individual state. Numerous valuable lessons could be developed by making comparisons and analyzing trends during the 70-year period for which data are provided.

[Inter-university Consortium for Political and Social Research]

Comment	**Historical Documents** gopher://vax.queens.lib.ny.us/11[gopher._ss._histdocs] The full text of the following documents related to United States history can be readily accessed and downloaded from this site. Declaration of Independence Emancipation Proclamation Gettysburg Address Jefferson's First Inaugural Address (1801) Lincoln's Second Inaugural Address (1865) Magna Carta Martin Luther King's "I Have a Dream" (1963) Mayflower Compact Monroe Doctrine Nelson Mandela's Inauguration Speech (1994) The United States Constitution Washington's Farewell Address (1796) [Queens Library, New York City]
Comment	**History as a Career** http://www.tntech.edu/www/acad/hist/career.html Although this site includes much useful information about conducting job searches, its main purpose is to explore the career options for an individual with history degrees. [Department of History, Tennessee Technological University]
Comment	**History Channel** http://www.historychannel.com/index2.html A rich resource of teaching tips, activities, study guides, and classroom materials to accompany cable television's outstanding History Channel programs. Teachers have permission to videotape the History Channel programs and use them for up to one year. Past programs may also be purchased rather inexpensively. "This Day in History" provides a searchable database of noted historical events which occurred on each day of the year. Post the day's historical anniversaries on the bulletin board or on an overhead as a great interest-arousing feature for history classes. [The History Channel. A&E Television Networks]

History Net

Comment

http://www.thehistorynet.com/

This topnotch megasite, a history buff's view of paradise, is filled with material on all aspects of world and American history. The "Today in History" section features dozens of historical events which occurred on each day of the year; useful for posting on bulletin board displays. The "History Net Archives" is stocked with a multitude of fascinating links filed under the following categories:

> Eyewitness Accounts
> Personality Profiles
> Great Battles of the Ages
> Arms, Armies, and Intrigue
> Interviews
> Historic Travel
> Aviation and Technology
> Homes and Heritage

[American Historical Society]

Historical Maps of the United States

Comment

http://www.lib.utexas.edu/Libs/PCL/Map_collection/histus.html

An online collection of historical maps records the territorial growth, distribution of early Indian tribes, exploration and settlement of the United States.

[The Perry-Castañeda Library Map Collection, The University of Texas at Austin]

The HistoryNet: American History

Comment

A+

http://www.thehistorynet.com/THNarchives/AmericanHistory/

Bookmark this site. It is a winner, filled with well-researched, articulate articles covering a wide range of American history topics. The frequently updated site includes special interviews, eyewitness accounts, personality profiles, noteworthy battles, and book reviews. Just a small sampling of the current articles posted here:

> 1797: The First Real Election
> Airmail's First Day
> Blue Ridge Traditions

Civil War Railroads
Ex-Slave Mary Fields Felt at Home in Montana
The Humble Undertaker
The Negro Leagues: How Good Were They?
Personality: Henry Ford
Walk-A-Heaps: Black Infantrymen in the West

[National Historical Society]

History Online

Comment

http://www.discovery.com/area/history/history.html

A monthly feature of cable television's Discovery Channel, this electronic magazine offers an archive of fascinating, seldom-told stories, from Warren G. Harding's extramarital adventures, and Mathew Brady's rise as one of the nineteenth century's greatest photographers, to the premiere of the first bikini. Enter the multimedia exhibit, "The Day of the Black Blizzard," to discover what it was really like to survive a 1930s Kansas dust storm, an era when women learned to knead dough in drawers only open wide enough to slip in their hands, lest the dough become coated with dust. The fabric of history lessons can be enriched and enlivened with the colorful and poignant stories offered at this pleasantly designed Web site.

[The Discovery Channel]

How the Other Half Lives

Comment

http://www.cis.yale.edu/amstud/inforev/riis/title.html

David Phillips has painstakingly edited Jacob Riis's important exposé *How the Other Half Lives: Studies among the Tenements of New York*, first published in 1890. Phillips' hypertext edition includes all the riveting illustrations from the original print edition of Riis' book. The text and images are in the public domain and Mr. Phillips kindly grants permission to reproduce his hypertext edition for nonprofit use by teachers.

[David Phillips]

Invention Dimension

Comment

http://web.mit.edu/invent/

What does it take to be an inventor? What is the most important invention we could not live without? The hair blower, automobile, or personal computer? These questions asked of 1,000 American adults were addressed in "The Invention

Index," a national survey on inventions and inventors. There is much in this worthwhile resource on inventions and inventors that will spark the interest of your students.

[Lemelson-MIT Prize Program, Massachusetts Institute of Technology]

Iroquois Constitution

Comment

http://www.law.uoknor.edu/iroquois.html

The full text of the Iroquois Constitution includes sections on Duties and Rights of War, Official Symbolism, Laws of Emigration, Rights of the People of the Five Nations, Protection of the House, and Funeral Addresses.

[The University of Oklahoma Law Center]

Jackie Robinson: Beyond the Playing Field

Comment

http://www.nara.gov/education/teaching/robinson/robmain.html

Jackie Robinson, the first black man to "officially" play in the big leagues, became a civil rights advocate after he retired from the game. The National Archives has assembled a set of ten lessons using primary documents which will prove valuable in teaching about civil rights, character education, and citizenship. For example, one item is a 1958 letter from Jackie Robinson to President Eisenhower seeking the President's support and action in providing blacks their due civil rights.

[National Archives and Records Administration]

Jewish-American Civil War Documents

Comment

http://home.earthlink.net/~lberk/jewish.htm

A letter home from a Jewish Confederate soldier describing how he and his brother observed Passover is but one of the enlightening documents housed in this unique archive. Because so rarely is the participation of Jewish persons included in coverage of the American Civil War, most students will probably be surprised to discover their role in both the North and South. A small sample of the treasures to be found here:

> "Bible View of Slavery" by Rabbi Morris J. Raphall
> Union Passover
> Civil War Letters of Rabbi Arnold Fischel, Chaplain
> Letter of Robert E. Lee to Rabbi Michelbacher of "Beth

Ahabah"
Bibliography of sources about Jewish Americans in the Civil War

[Leah Berkowitz]

Korean War

Comment

http://www.onramp.net/~hbarker/

This conflict has become all but forgotten in most American history classes. The "Overview of the Korean War" section from the Army Historical Series, *American Military History,* provides a good general background of the war, albeit from the vantage point of the U.S. military. A detailed set of colorful, informative maps can be downloaded. Diaries of veterans and contemporary newspaper accounts add a richness to the content that can't be fully gleaned from a standard history book.

[Hal Barker and Ted Barker, Korean War Project]

Letters Home: A War Memoir (Europe 1944-1945)

Comment

http://www.pagesz.net/~jbdavis/ww2_ausland.html

John Ausland, who landed at Normandy on D-Day and fought in Europe for the duration of the war with Germany, wrote a book chronicling his war experiences. This book can be accessed chapter by chapter. Letters home, some photographs, and a series of articles Mr. Ausland wrote for the *International Herald Tribune* are also available. Sample chapters:

> The 4th Lands in Normandy
> The Final Preparation for D-Day
> Operation COBRA and Breakout
> The Liberation of Paris
> Ernest Hemingway and Ernie Pyle with the 4th
> The 4th Helps Push Back the German Offensive
> The Allies Are Suspicious of Each Other
> The War Is Finally Over
> The 4th Division Returns to The U.S.

[John Davis, Keeping The Memory Alive]

Martin Luther King, Jr. World Wide Web Site

Comment

http://www-leland.stanford.edu/group/King/

This site provides access to materials by and about the civil rights leader, including King's most important speeches. Users are required to complete a free registration form to view copyrighted material, including Dr. King's "I Have a Dream" speech. The King estate has been very vigilant in enforcing copyright restrictions on use of the King speeches and pictures. To be on the safe side, it would be wise to seek permission before using any of its materials.

[Martin Luther King, Jr. Center in Atlanta; Martin Luther King, Jr. Papers Project at Stanford]

A+

Comment

Mayflower Web Pages

http://members.aol.com/calebj/mayflower.html

The meticulous research of this Web site's author is evident. Carefully documented narratives on topics such as "Girls on the Mayflower," "Pilgrim Clothing," and "History and Foods of the First Thanksgiving" elevate this historic event beyond a list of names or dates. Full text editions of several historical documents related to the Mayflower and the lives of the passengers and their descendants should provide worthwhile teaching content. The site's author does grant permission to teachers to duplicate material from his pages for use in their classrooms. A few of the outstanding items included:

> Common Myths
> Mourt's Relation: A Journal of the Pilgrims at Plymouth
> The History of the Ship
> Probate Inventory Done on the Mayflower, 1624
> Weapons and Armor of the Pilgrims
> Bradford's Journal, Of Plymouth Plantation
> John Pory's Description of the Plymouth Colony

[Caleb Johnson]

Comment

Medicinal Uses of Plants by Native Americans

http://probe.nalusda.gov:8300/cgi-bin/browse/mpnadb

The Iroquois used wild carrot (or Queen Anne's lace) as a dietary aid to stimulate appetite, and Cherokees mixed blackberries and honey to soothe a sore throat. A huge database of plants can be searched for the medical uses by Native Americans. An unusual, no-frills, but fascinating, Web site maintained by the U.S. Department of Agriculture. What this resource lacks in splashy graphics it makes up for in the richness of its content.

[U.S. Department of Agriculture]

Comment

Mexican-American War

http://sunsite.unam.mx/revistas/1847/Summa.html

What makes this online exhibit unique is that it is created from the Mexican perspective. Overall, the treatment of the subject seems to be fair and reasonably impartial. Several outstanding primary resources, particularly a noteworthy firsthand account of an American soldier who participated in the war, are included in the exhibit. As this Web site is a translation of the Spanish version, a few more typographical errors remain than might normally be expected.

[Universidad Nacional Autónoma de México]

Military History

Comment

http://160.147.68.21:80/cmh-pg/

Where else would you find a December 7, 1941 map of Pearl Harbor or a copy of "Black Soldier, White Army: The 24th Infantry in Korea"? The U.S. Army's official site includes a huge number of original documents and links to dozens of others covering the span of U.S. military affairs from 1776 to the present.

[Center of Military History]

Mount Vernon Educational Resource

Comment

http://www.mountvernon.org/education/

The official Web site of George Washington's historic home presents a variety of educational resources about the President's magnificent estate and its famous occupant. View the 1799 census of slaves, completed shortly before George Washington's death, or complete the George Washington Quiz to test your knowledge of the nation's first president.

[Mount Vernon Estate & Gardens]

National Air and Space Museum

Comment

http://www.nasm.edu/NASMDOCS/NASMAP_96.html

A picture-filled virtual tour depicts all the major displays of the Smithsonian's National Air and Space Museum. Each major event in the development and history of aviation and space exploration is told with well-written text and pleasing graphics.

[Smithsonian Institution]

Comment	## National Museum of the American Indian
	
	http://www.si.edu/nmai/abmus.htm
	
	This online taste of the Smithsonian's Museum of the American Indian highlights current exhibits on the life, history, languages, arts, and literature of Native Americans. Each Web page is overflowing with excellent content, beautiful photographs and graphics, and concise descriptive text. As the exhibits are frequently changed, it is worth checking back frequently. Regularly updated links to additional Native American sites are also maintained. A sampling of current exhibits:
	
	    Stories of the People
	    Creation's Journey: Masterworks of Native American
	    Identity and Belief
	    Woven by the Grandmothers: Nineteenth-Century Navajo
	    Textiles
	    Fiddle Album
	
	[The Smithsonian Institution]

Comment	## Native Languages Page http://www.pitt.edu/~lmitten/natlang.html Links from this clearinghouse will permit you to download a Cherokee font, learn the Dakota language, study Navajo words, obtain statistics on native language speakers in the U.S. and Canada, or hear words in Osage, Cherokee, Wyandotte, Choctaw, or Ft. Sill Apache. [Lisa Mittenat, University of Pittsburgh]

Comment	## New Deal Network
	
	http://newdeal.marist.edu/
	
	Dedicated to exploring the events, achievements, and personalities associated with the New Deal, this electronic archive provides an extensive collection of useful teaching resources. A small collection of lesson plans related to the New Deal is maintained. The clearinghouse includes numerous items under each of the following categories:
	
	    Cultural Programs (e.g.—murals and paintings, sculptures, art centers, plays, theaters, orchestras, bands)
	    Construction Projects (e.g.—bridges, highways, traffic tunnels, subways, airports, ships, waterworks, dams, sewage

systems, schools, libraries, prisons, fire stations, historical restorations)

Social Programs (e.g.—adult education, educational radio, disease prevention, youth centers, museum work, maps and charts)

New Deal Era (photos, celebrities, the Roosevelts, unemployment, disasters)

[Franklin and Eleanor Roosevelt Institute, Franklin D. Roosevelt Library and Museum, Marist College, and IBM Corporation]

New World Slavery

Comment

http://vi.uh.edu/pages/mintz/gilder.htm

Firsthand accounts from a variety of perspectives describe the "peculiar institution" as it evolved in North America over two and a half centuries. Poignant, personal accounts are preserved in this noteworthy archive.

A small sample of the documents available through this site:

A European slave trader, John Barbot, describes the African slave trade (1682)

Olaudah Equiano, an 11-year-old boy from Nigeria, remembers his kidnapping into slavery (1789)

A European slave trader, James Bardot, Jr., describes a shipboard revolt by enslaved Africans (1700)

An English physician, Alexander Falconbridge, describes the treatment of newly arrived slaves in the West Indies (1788)

Solomon Northrup describes the working conditions of slaves on a Louisiana cotton plantation (1853)

Josiah Henson describes slave housing, diet, and clothing (1877)

James W. C. Pennington analyzes the impact of slavery upon childhood (1849)

Frederick Douglass describes the circumstances that prompted masters to whip slaves (1845)

Frederick Douglass resists a slave breaker (1845)

Nat Turner describes his revolt against slavery (1831)

Harriet Tubman sneaks into the South to free slaves (1863, 1865)

Colonel Samuel Thomas describes the attitudes of ex-Confederates toward the freed men

[The Gilder Lehrman Institute of American History]

Comment	### Paul Cowan's Quotes List http://www.access.digex.net/~bdboyle/quotes.html "It is well that war is so terrible, lest we grow too fond of it," quipped Robert E. Lee to Lt. Gen. Longstreet at the Battle of Fredericksburg. This is but one of a group of 77 noted Civil War era quotations assembled by the late Paul Cowan. One of his favorite Abe Lincoln quotes was, "The best thing about the future is that it comes only one day at a time." [Stephen Schmidt, Department of Economics, Union College]

Comment	### Pictures of the Civil War
	
	http://gopher.nara.gov:70/0h/inform/dc/audvis/still/civwar.html
	
	Photographic images from the War Between the States include photographs from the Mathew B. Brady collection and from the War Department Library. They are clustered under four main headings:
	
	   Activities (army life, civilians, engineering, medical, navies, prisoners)
	   Places (battle sites, Richmond, Washington, D.C.)
	   Portraits (Abolitionists, Union and Confederate officers, officials, women)
	   Lincoln's assassination (assassins, Ford's Theater)
	
	[National Archives and Records Administration]

Comment	### Plymouth and the Pilgrims http://media3.com/plymouth/index.htm Although designed as a travel promotional piece, this Web site does include enough information about the history of Plymouth Colony to be worthy of an online visit. The true story of "The First Thanksgiving" and the New England style recipes could stimulate November lesson ideas. A virtual tour of "Plimoth Plantation" is the next best thing to being there. [Destination Plymouth, The Plymouth Area Chamber of Commerce, Pilgrims World]

Comment	**Politics in the Valley of the Shadow** http://jefferson.village.Virginia.EDU/vshadow2/outlines/politics. html A firsthand account of local politics in pre-Civil War Virginia through an extensive collection of articles from three nineteenth-century newspapers. *The Republican Vindicator* and *Valley Spirit* reflect a Democratic leaning, while the *Staunton Spectator* tended to support the opposition, originally the Whigs. A fantastic primary resource including keyword search capabilities for gleaning contemporary perspectives of John Brown's Raid, daily family life, Lincoln's election, religion, race relations, secession, and military life. [University of Virginia research project]
Comment	**Presidents** http://sunsite.unc.edu/lia/president/ This virtual gateway to the past features links to all the Presidential libraries and Web sites for each of the Presidents and First Ladies. A good place to start in researching the lives, policies, and achievements of any of the U.S. Presidents. [Leadership Information Archives, University of North Carolina]
Comment	**Presidents of the United States** http://www.ipl.org/ref/POTUS/ Who was the only President who studied to become a doctor? Which President later served as Chief Justice of the United States? The answers to these and many other questions are answered in this thorough and inviting Web site. Each hypertext Presidential listing includes biographical information, previous offices, Presidential election results, cabinet members, Presidential highlights, links to related historical documents, and audio clips of most twentieth-century Presidents. A bountiful cornucopia of Presidential tidbits and memorabilia. [Robert S. Summers]
Comment	**Primary Sources and Activities** http://www.nara.gov/education/teaching/teaching.html

A small but valuable reference on using primary documents in teaching United States history and government. Be sure to check out its sample lesson plans, with downloadable copies of primary documents from the National Archives. Lessons available:

> Jackie Robinson: Beyond the Playing Field
> The Zimmermann Telegram, 1917
> Constitutional Issues: Separation of Powers
> Constitutional Issues: Watergate and the Constitution

[National Archives and Records Administration]

Radio Days

Comment

http://www.otr.com/

If you have RealAudio software, you can relive the early days of radio, when it was the thing to do on Saturday night. Users can download or play clips from early radio programs and news events. Embellish history classes with soundbites related to the topic of the day. Try any of these to enliven your lessons:

> NBC Radio announces the first bulletin about Pearl Harbor attack
> Neville Chamberlain announces that England is at war with Germany
> German Radio announces the death of Adolf Hitler

[James F. Widner]

Rare Map Collection

Comment

http://www.libs.uga.edu/darchive/hargrett/maps/maps.html

About one-fifth of the university's special collection of 800 historical maps is stored as JPEG files (average size is 400K) which can be viewed online. Organized by time periods, the maps cover the New World, Colonial America, The American Civil War, and the Nineteenth Century. Many Georgia maps are included. You must get permission before reproducing any of the images, so send an e-mail message making such requests.

[The University of Georgia Libraries]

Re: Vietnam—Stories Since the War

Comment

http://www.pbs.org/pov/stories/

This rich repository of oral history, reflections, and hopes features stories and comments from volunteer contributors. Touching anecdotes, essays, interviews, and letters have been added by people affected by the Vietnam War: veterans, draft-dodgers, government officials, war protesters, families and friends of those lost in the war.

[PBS Online and P.O.V. Interactive]

Sixties Project

Comment   http://jefferson.village.Virginia.EDU/sixties/

A holistic, scholarly look at this unique period in American history, The Sixties Project provides links to an assortment of primary and secondary sources related to the 1960s and the Vietnam Era. Though the site is under construction, the most valued features currently are the syllabi of college courses relating to the era's literature, culture, film, and history. A keyword search engine facilitates access to thousands of pages of Internet links related to this era. An enhanced, user-friendly index facilitates browsing.

[Institute of Advanced Technology in Humanities at University of Virginia—Charlottesville and Viet Nam Generation, Inc.]

Sullivan Ballou Letter

Comment   http://ac.acusd.edu/History/text/civilwar/ballou.html

A week before the Battle of Bull Run, a major in the 2nd Rhode Island Volunteers wrote this touching letter to his wife. He died in that battle. The recitation of this letter was a memorable segment of Ken Burns' PBS Civil War series and resulted in a subsequent 15-minute film production, *The Sullivan Ballou Letter*.

[The Sullivan Ballou Film Project]

Teaching with Historic Places

Comment   http://www.cr.nps.gov/nr/twhp/home.html

Most communities have one or more structures listed with the National Register of Historic Places. These structures can be used to help students better understand American history, geography, and civics and to enrich their awareness of the man-made environment. This site provides lesson plans and other publications for teachers. A free "Author's Packet" facilitates constructing lesson plans for students from upper elementary to high school.

[National Register of Historic Places]

Vietnam War

Comment

ftp://ftp.msstate.edu/docs/history/USA/Vietnam/vietnam.html

Through text and photographs the history of the Vietnam War is preserved. Though a limited amount of original material is housed here, important links to pictorial archives, songs of the Vietnam War, historical accounts, and casualty statistics are included.

[Mississippi State University]

War News from Iowa Soldiers

Comment

http://www.alaska.net/~design/civilwar/index.html

A poignant view of the Civil War through the letters, photos, and diary of the McNeal family soldiers from Keokuk County, Iowa.

[Larry Pearson]

Westward Ho!

Comment

http://town.pvt.k12.ca.us/Collaborations/WWHO/tresources.html

Created by two teachers, this cooperative learning simulation leads students through a five-week journey along the Oregon Trail. Interactive participation among students is required to complete the adventure. Each year, teachers are invited to register their classes and join the Westward Ho! Wagon Train. En route the adventurers are required to make a variety of "life or death" decisions which influence their chance of arriving safely. Participating teachers can share teaching ideas in the weekly online meetings. These electronic conferences are a unique and powerful feature of this learning experience, permitting teachers to tap into the creativity of fellow online teachers. This is truly an innovative and engaging educational experience. Check it out.

[Kathleen Ferenz, Leni Donlan, and Paula Polly]

Comment	### Women Come to the Front http://lcweb.loc.gov/exhibits/wcf/wcf0001.html This splendid online exhibit from the folks at the Library of Congress highlights the experiences of female journalists, photographers, and broadcasters who served in World War II. Eight women and their work in the war are featured. [Library of Congress]
Comment	### Women in America, 1820-1842 http://xroads.virginia.edu/~HYPER/DETOC/FEM/home.htm In the 1820-1842 era, eighteen travelers from Ireland, Germany, Scotland, England, and France recorded their observations of American life, including the role of women. The documents preserved in this site examine courtship, marriage, employment, education, the arts, health, fashion, religion, Indians, and race. [Mary Halnon]
Comment	### Women's Suffrage http://lcweb2.loc.gov/ammem/rbnawsahtml/nawshom.html Another fine Library of Congress exhibit, "Selections from the National American Woman Suffrage Association, 1848-1921," traces the struggle of women to secure the right to vote from the first U.S. women's rights convention at Seneca Falls, New York, to the ratification of the Nineteenth Amendment. Full-text articles by the movement's leaders are enhanced with illustrations. Instructions are included for downloading special software needed to view the graphic images. [Library of Congress]
Comment	### Working On The Railroad http://www.mcs.net/~dsdawdy/cyberoad.html If you love trains, you will cherish this resource, which includes anything and everything about the history and operation of railroads. This archive, sponsored by Cyberspace World Railroad & Association of American Railroads, is laden with valuable articles, photographs, and announcements. Past features and connections include:

Canadian Railway News
Animation File on How Trains Stop
"ODDITIES"—Things I Photograph Along the Rails That
Most People Don't!
New & Updated Fonts for the PC and MAC Are Here From
Benn Coifman
Conrail Newsletter
Locomotive Driving Course
Canadian National CN Corporation Corporate Home Page
Union Pacific Corporate Home Page

A jumplist to other railroad-related Web sites is available to those who just can't get enough. It appears to be updated weekly, so check back often.

[Ribbon Rail Productions]

A+

World War II: Keeping the Memory Alive

Comment

http://www.pagesz.net/~jbdavis/

This online archive houses a number of poignant first-person accounts of World War II. Most of the items are original documents, not merely links to other sites. Useful teaching resources include a sizable collection of photographs, letters and diaries, ocean liners of World War II, and war-related documents and speeches. It is most commendable that one person has assumed the responsibility of preserving and making such a historical treasure available to millions of Internet users. A jumplist to other World War II-related sites is included.

[John Davis]

World War II—"50 Years Ago" Archives

Comment

http://www.webcom.com/~jbd/ww2.html

A Web site devoted to keeping the memory of World War II alive. John Davis writes a daily column, "50 Years Ago," which reports on the events of World War II, both on the battlefronts and on the American homefront.

All previously published "50 Years Ago" articles and a wide assortment of World War II-related items, including a vast collection of photographs, are readily available through this site. First-person accounts of veterans and Web connections to a plethora of World War II-related sites are also available through this source.

This World Wide Web page includes these special collections:

> "50 Years Ago" Bulletin Board
> World War II Photograph Collection
> World War II Picture Album
> Memories Of World War II
> Cornelius Ryan Collection
> U.S.S. Wahoo (SS-238) War Patrol Reports
> Documents And Speeches
> U.S.S. Juneau (CL-52) War Diary

ELECTRONIC MAILING LISTS: AMERICAN HISTORY

Many electronic mailing lists focus on topics of interest to U.S. history teachers and students. Subscribing is easy. For example, to subscribe to the mailing list H-AMREL on American religious history:

Send an e-mail message to: LISTSERV@H-NET.MSU.EDU

Usually it is best to leave the "Subject" line blank. If your e-mail software requires something in the subject line simply type a period.

Enter the message: subscribe H-AMREL John Doe

The format for the message is: subscribe <List_Name> <Your_Full_Name>

Caerleon
Ideas for hands-on history lessons
E-mail to: LISTPROC@U.WASHINGTON.EDU

Civil
American Civil War Newsletter
E-mail to: MAJORDOMO@LISTSERV.PRODIGY.COM

H-Amrel
American religious history
E-mail to: LISTSERV@H-NET.MSU.EDU

H-Amstdy
American studies
E-mail to: LISTSERV@UICVM.UIC.EDU

H-ASEH
American Society for Environmental History
E-mail to: LISTSERV@H-NET.MSU.EDU

H-Civwar
United States Civil War forum
E-mail to: LISTSERV@H-NET.MSU.EDU

H-Costume

History of clothing
E-mail to: H-COSTUME-REQUEST2ANDREW.CMU.EDU

H-Labor

Labor history discussion forum
E-mail to: LISTSERV@H-NET.MSU.EDU

H-Shear

History of the Early American Republic
E-mail to: LISTSERV@KSUVM.KSU.EDU

H-Shgape

History of the Gilded Age and Progressive Era
E-mail to: LISTSERV@H-NET.MSU.EDU

H-South

History of the American South
E-mail to: LISTSERV@H-NET.MSU.EDU

H-Teach

Forum for college history teachers
E-mail to: LISTSERV@H-NET.MSU.EDU

H-Uurban

Urban history
E-mail to: LISTSERV@H-NET.MSU.EDU

H-West

History of the American West
E-mail to: LISTSERV@H-NET.MSU.EDU

Ieahcnet

American colonial history
E-mail to: LISTSERV@UICVM.UIC.EDU

Iroqec-L

Native American issues
E-mail to: LISTSERV@UBVM.BITNET

Memories

Students can interact with WWII survivors
E-mail to: LISTSERV@SJUVM.STJOHNS.EDU

Prezhist

History of U.S. Presidents
E-mail to: LISTSERV@KASEY.UMKC.EDU

Sixties-L
Interdisciplinary forum on the 1960s
E-mail to: LISTPROC@JEFFERSON.VILLAGE.VIRGINIA.EDU

Tamha
Teaching American History
E-mail to: LISTSERV@CMS.CC.WAYNE.EDU

Newsgroups: American History

alt.history.living	Survivors of historical events discussion
alt.history.what-if	Alternate history conjecture
alt.war.civil.usa	Anything on the U.S. Civil War
alt.war.korea	Korean War events and recollections
alt.war.vietnam	Vietnam War discussion
soc.history	Miscellaneous discussions on history
soc.history.moderated	Moderated history forum
soc.history.war.us-civil-war	Civil War forum
soc.history.war.us-revolution	The American Revolution
soc.history.war.vietnam	Vietnam War
soc.history.war.world-war-ii	Events of World War II
talk.politics.misc	Miscellaneous political discussion
talk.politics.theory	Assorted political theories

Section 4

WORLD HISTORY

Best Web Sites: World History

Comment	**African Art: Aesthetics and Meaning** http://www.lib.virginia.edu/dic/exhib/93.ray.aa/African.html This electronic exhibition catalog features a sampling of African sculpture, masks, and headdresses with vivid color photographs and descriptive text. The next best thing to being there. [Bayly Art Museum, University of Virginia]

Comment	**Ancient Egypt**
	
	http://www.library.nwu.edu/class/history/B94/
	
	Who were the ancient Egyptians? What was their world like? What impact did their civilization have on our world today? These are but a few of the questions addressed by this extensive repository of resources illustrating the history of ancient Egypt. In addition to much text material, images of geographical features and archealogical remains of the Nile Valley embellish the content of this excellent site. This splendid Web site was created for Professor Peter Piccione's History of Ancient Egypt course. The main topics covered in his course and on this electronic link:
	
	    Chronology of Egyptian Civilization
	    A Relative Chronology of Nubia and Egypt, 8000 BC-1600 AD
	    Excursus: Basin Irrigation in Egypt
	    Excursus II: Egyptian and the Afro-Asiatic Languages
	    Excursus III: The Status of Women in Ancient Egyptian Society
	    Excursus IV: Nubia: The Land Upriver
	    Names, Places, and Words to Remember
	    Visuals and Images Utilized in Class
	    Internet Resources
	    Background Information
	    Finding Books
	
	[Northwestern University Library]

Comment	**Ancient Medicine / Medicina Antiqua** http://www.ea.pvt.k12.pa.us/medant/ Discover how the Ancient Greek healers used a person's dreams to aid in diagnosis. An unusual, but interesting, resource features English translations of medical advice from Hippocrates and other Greek and Roman physicians. [Dr. Lee T. Pearcy, The Episcopal Academy]

Comment	**Anglo-Saxon England** http://www.phoenix.net/~melanie/anglo-sa.htm A great resource for anyone interested in the Anglo-Saxon era of England's history. Major sections include: Anglo-Saxon Kings Anglo-Saxon Writings Timeline of Anglo-Saxon England Anglo-Saxon Links Select Bibliography [Pel Mel Productions]
Comment	**Antique Roman Dishes** http://www.mit.edu:8001/people/wchuang/cooking/recipes/Roman/Ancient_Roman.html Had any aliter baedinam sive agninam excaldatam lately? That was steamed lamb for the ancient Romans. This site features a variety of recipes from the Roman kitchens. Don't worry; all are in English. Interesting reading, even if they aren't tasted. [Micaela Pantke]
Comment	**Atomic Archive** http://sd.znet.com/~ajsftwre/AtomicAge.html With the decline of communism, less is heard of the "Nuclear Age" and its accouterments, such as atomic bomb drills in U.S. schools and home bomb shelters. Through hypertext, photographs, video clips, and historical documents, the escalation of the atomic age is superbly depicted in this thought-provoking electronic archive. [AJ Software & Multimedia]
Comment	**Biography** http://www.biography.com/ The online edition of A&E television's "Biography" series features reviews of the current top-selling biographies, the weekly Biography Quiz, Biography Anagrams, upcoming program listings, and access to 15,000 biographies through the Cambridge Biographical Encyclopedia. Videotapes of

previous "Biography" programs are available for purchase (most for under $20).

[A&E Entertainment]

British Monarchy

Comment

http://www.royal.gov.uk/

The official Web site of the British monarchy won't provide much information about the royal family, but almost everything else about the palaces, succession to the throne, official press releases, and the royal collection of art, jewels, and treasures will be found in the 150 pages of this tastefully done electronic exhibit. A few gems to be found at the monarch's Web site:

Accession, coronation, and succession
Today's Royal family
Your questions answered
Press releases
Links to other sites

[British Royal Family]

Buddhism

Comment

http://coombs.anu.edu.au/WWWVL-Buddhism.html

Two Australian professors have selected the most authoritative Internet resources on Buddhist studies for inclusion in this large and useful clearinghouse. Structured for optimal transmission speed rather than elegant appearance, the collection is updated continuously.

[Dr. T. Matthew Ciolek and Dr. John C. Powers, Australian National University]

Canadian Historical Documents

Comment

http://schoolnet.carleton.ca/cdisk/CanadiskTextBase/
CanadiskTextBase.html

From the 1794 U.S.-Six Nations Treaty to the 1995 Quebec Referendum, dozens of Canadian historical documents are available through this virtual archive. The items are well organized in distinct categories, such as: British Documents, Native & Aboriginal, Documents Relating to Canadian Society, and World War II Documents.

[The SchoolNet Support Group]

Comment	### Canadiana http://www.cs.cmu.edu/Web/Unofficial/Canadiana/README.html The Canadian Resource Page is a virtual encyclopedia on every aspect of Canada, its history, geography, economy, politics, and culture. Approximately 500 links to information on Canadian history and genealogy can be found here. [Stewart M. Clamen, Carnegie Mellon University]
Comment	### Costumes http://www.siue.edu/COSTUMES/history.html How did costumes of the Roman soldiers differ from those of their Greek counterparts? What did the ancient Egyptian kings wear? How about the common folk of the same period? The "History of Costume," originally printed 1861 to 1880, contains 500 costume designs from antiquity to the end of the nineteenth century. Graphics and descriptive text illustrate the apparel of noblemen and women as well as the less-well-to-do from antiquity to the 1880 contemporaries of Europe, Africa, and America. [C. Otis Sweezey]
Comment	### Crossroads of Continents http://nmnhwww.si.edu/arctic/features/croads/ Complete a spectacular virtual tour of Northeastern Siberia, Alaska, and the remote and rough region linking the continents of Eurasia and North America. The multimedia exhibit emphasizes the spectrum of North Pacific cultures and their history from the end of the last Ice Age to the present. Audio and movie software will need to be installed on your browser to take full advantage of the exhibits. [Smithsonian Institution]
Comment	### Cultures of the Andes http://www.andes.org/ In the Quechu Indian language the idiom "Sonsochakoq" means "acting dumb." Music, photographs, poetry, and stories from the Andes mountain region of South America provide an intimate glimpse of the region's cultural heritage.

The songs are in Spanish or the Quechua Indian language. A page of additional Andean links is included.

[Ada & Russ Gibbons]

Dead Sea Scrolls

Comment

http://sunsite.unc.edu/expo/deadsea.scrolls.exhibit/intro.html

Are the Dead Sea Scrolls authentic? Who put them there and when? The Ancient Library of Qumran and Modern Scholarship, a Library of Congress exhibit, addresses these challenging questions. Images of 12 scroll fragments and 29 other objects are featured in this inviting online exhibit. The "Resource Materials for Teachers" section lists additional resources of value in teaching about the Dead Sea Scrolls.

[Library of Congress]

Decade magazine

Comment

http://www.sjen.org/esuhsd/curix/team31/DecadeMag.html

This creative high school history/English lesson plan encourages student teams to research and design a magazine about the 1940s. Students organize and present articles and illustrations in an interesting format. This lesson plan lists the specific items which must be included in each magazine project: a colorful cover and cover story, man or woman of the decade, critique of a play, the major scientific advancements of the decade, a timeline, interviews, an editorial, and feature articles on items such as sports, entertainment, fashions, and lifestyles. An excellent active learning strategy.

[San Jose Education Network]

DefenseLINK

Comment

http://www.dtic.mil/defenselink

How many missiles does a nuclear-powered submarine carry and how large is its crew? Discover the answer to this and many more questions through the DefenseLINK. The Pentagon has amassed a virtual ton of information about the U.S. defense establishment, the organization of the military, its military hardware, and world events.

[U.S. Department of Defense]

	Distinguished Women of the Past and Present
Comment	http://www.netsrq.com/~dbois/
	Brief biographies of women who have had a significant impact on world culture are organized in 34 categories, from agriculture to stage and screen. The hundreds of notables, some long dead, others still living, range from Sakajawe, the Shoshone Native American interpreter and guide of the Lewis and Clark expedition, to Mother Teresa of Calcutta. The collection is categorized into those living before 1900 and those born during the twentieth century. The biographies are linked from various resources and vary in format and length.
	[Danuta Bois]
	Duke Papyrus Archive
Comment	http://odyssey.lib.duke.edu/papyrus/texts/homepage.html
	This serious academic repository offers electronic images of 1,373 papyri from ancient Egypt. Of course, unless you can read Hieratic, Demotic, Coptic, Greek, or Latin, you won't be able to interpret any of those documents, but most students (or teachers) have never seen real papyrus documents. Apart from the digitized images of every type (e.g., religious documents, letters, tax accounts, wills, horoscopes), there is ample English text to illuminate every aspect of papyrology. Truly a glimpse of paradise for Coptologists, Egyptologists, biblical scholars, and papyrologists. Interesting fodder for just plain folks, too.
	[Special Collections Library, Duke University]
	Early Church Documents
Comment	http://www.iclnet.org/pub/resources/christian-history.html
	This extensive hypertext guide contains links to Web sites containing early Christian church historical documents. The section on dating of the books of the Bible provides an educational insight into the scholarly study of the Christian religion.
	[John Brubaker and Gary Bogart, Institute for Christian Leadership]

Comment	## Eighteenth-Century Resources on the Net http://www.english.upenn.edu/~jlynch/18th/ This electronic clearinghouse provides links to hundreds of sources related to the eighteenth century: revolutions in America and France, the minuet, powdered wigs for men, and the literature of Keats and Milton. Items are arranged in the following categories: literature, history, art, music, religion, economics, science and technology, and philosophy. The collection has a European-North American bent, with special emphasis on British literature. [Jack Lynch, University of Pennsylvania]
Comment	## Electronic Renaissance http://www.idbsu.edu:80/courses/hy309/visitor.html This innovative online college-level course utilizes hypertext documents and links, Bitnet list discussions, and assigned outside readings. The course provides an excellent introduction to the Italian Renaissance and the history of Europe from approximately 1300 to 1500. Discussion questions, essays, outside links, and references make this a valuable resource for any world history teacher. With the exception of the maps, which are copyrighted by a separate source, the site creator generously grants permission to use the course materials in the classroom. [Dr. E. L. Skip Knox, Boise State University]
Comment	## Encyclopedia of Women's History http://www.teleport.com/~megaines/women.html "Written by and for the K12 community" as a school project by students in grades 3 through 12, these entries were posted as written, without editing for content or grammar. The sponsor notes that English was a second language for some students. The value of this site is less as an academic reference than as a model of what can be done using the Internet as a motivational tool. [Portland Jewish Academy]

	EuroDocs: Primary Historical Documents From Western Europe
Comment	http://library.byu.edu/~rdh/eurodocs/
	Though constructed almost solely of links to other sites, the library includes a most comprehensive collection of primary resources covering the major political, cultural, and historical events in the development of Western Europe. The depth, breadth, and richness of these translations, facsimiles, and transcriptions make this a valuable reference for scholars and teachers.
	[Harold B. Lee Library, Brigham Young University]

A+

	Exploring Ancient World Cultures
Comment	http://eawc.evansville.edu/index.htm
	Designed by a worldwide team of scholars, this tastefully done electronic college-level textbook provides a fascinating introduction to ancient world cultures. Hypertext links connect students to a cornucopia of articles, pictures, maps, references, and quizzes. All world history teachers will find much of value here, even if their students do not have access to the Internet.
	[Anthony F. Beavers, Editor, Department of Philosophy and Religion. The University of Evansville]

	Gathering of the Clan
Comment	http://www.tartans.com/
	Devoted to all things Scottish, this Web server is filled with information on Scottish folklore, history, heraldry, and culture. The "Gaelic Cultural Centre" provides information on Scottish culture and the language of the Gaels. The "Great Hall of the Clans" yields an impressive selection of downloadable images of Scottish heraldry, including crests, badges, flags, tartans, and histories of many clans.
	[DISCscribe Ltd.]

Comment	**Greek Mythology** http://www.intergate.net/uhtml/.jhunt/greek_myth/greek_myth.html How did Zeus become the ruler of the gods? What role did Typhoeus, the fire-breathing dragon with a hundred heads, play? An Introduction to Ancient Greek Mythology attempts to answer these and other questions about the gods, heroes, creatures, and stories of Ancient Greece. [John M. Hunt]
Comment	**Handbook of Latin American Studies** http://lcweb2.loc.gov/hlas/ Updated monthly, this online version of the well-researched Library of Congress reference book is arguably the most useful, accurate, and up-to-date guide to Latin America. At this point the book does not provide links to any of these resources, most of which are published books or journal articles, which must still be located the old-fashioned way—by a visit to a real-world library. [Library of Congress]

Comment	**Hiroshima-Nagasaki Project**
	
	http://www.peacewire.org/pw/hiromenu.html
	
	In memory of those who perished in the bombing of Hiroshima and Nagasaki, this site focuses upon the use and proliferation of the atomic bomb. A listing of the countries currently possessing nuclear weapons and a nuclear photo gallery are also included. Among the related articles featured:
	
	    Forgetting the bomb, the assault on history
	    Was Hiroshima necessary to end the war?
	    Hiroshima: the first shot in the cold war
	    A long-range policy for nuclear forces of the nuclear powers
	
	[Peacewire]

Comment	**Historic Speeches** http://speeches.com/historic.html Links to text, audio, or video clips of the most notable speeches in world history are featured in this Web site. With

a couple of whimsical exceptions (e.g., Dan Quayle's speech panning the "Murphy Brown" television series), this is an admirable collection of history's greatest orations. Sample fare:

> Winston Churchill's "We shall defend our island whatever the cost" June 4, 1940 speech on the retreat from Flanders
> John Kennedy's Berlin speeches
> Martin Luther King, Jr.'s "I have a dream."
> Abraham Lincoln's "Gettysburg Address"

[David Slack Communications]

Comment

Historical Text Archive

http://www.msstate.edu/Archives/History/index.html

The creator of this site has done a great service for students, teachers, and historians by assembling digitized versions of numerous primary documents and texts related to world history. The documents are arranged by geographical region, as well as by topic. A sizable photo and map archive is also featured.

[Don Mabry, Mississippi State University]

Comment

Historical Women

http://www.inform.umd.edu/EdRes/Topic/WomensStudies/ReadingRoom/History/Biographies/

Biographies of dozens of noted women from many nations are included in this collection, though Americans are particularly represented. The women featured here range from Harriet Tubman and Marie Curie to Sandra Day O'Connor.

[University of Maryland]

A+

Comment

The HistoryNet: World History

http://www.thehistorynet.com/THNarchives/WorldHistory/

Bookmark this site. It is a winner, filled with well-researched, articulate articles covering a wide range of world history topics. The frequently updated site includes special interviews, eyewitness accounts, personality profiles, noteworthy battles, historic travels, and book reviews. Just a small sampling of the current articles posted here:

> The Bomb That Ended World War II

England's Warrior-King Edward I
The Great Fire of London
Losing Ground to the Khmer Rouge
Luftwaffe Ace Günther Rall Remembers
Stone Circles
The Traveling Circus
William Kidd's Last Voyage
Zulu Mountain Trap Sprung

[National Historical Society]

History of Medicine

Comment

http://oli.lhc.nlm.nih.gov/

Access a catalogued image archive of nearly 60,000 illustrations from the massive collection of the History of Medicine Division at the U.S. National Library of Medicine. Use keyword searches for specific topics or browse a selected sample of the images. An unusual exhibit of a topic often overlooked in history courses.

[U.S. National Library of Medicine]

History of Palestine

Comment

http://www.alquds.org/www/history/palestine.html

The history of this Middle East region is told through the eyes of the Palestinians. Featured historical documents include:

The Balfour Declaration
The British White Paper
The United Nations & Palestine
Israeli Laws
Hussein Ibn Ali & Sir Henry McMahon Letter Exchanges
Sykes Picot Agreement

[Palestine Information Center]

History of Printing

Comment

http://communication.ucsd.edu/bjones/Books/booktext.html

Before there was the Internet, there were printed books. The evolution of the printing press and ultimately printed books is detailed in this link-based historical account. The impact of the printed book and maps is expertly explored, detailing its influence upon the decline of the Roman Catholic Church and exploration of the New World.

[Bruce Jones, Department of Communication, University of California, San Diego]

	Holocaust
Comment	http://remember.org/
	First-person stories of Jews and non-Jews persecuted by the Nazis and true stories of young people who survived the Holocaust are only two of the many records featured in this powerful and poignant archive of the horrific Nazi experiment. The Virtual Tour of Auschwitz link provides a moving reminder of the brutality of this tragic experience. A multitude of teaching resources can be obtained through this Cybrary of the Holocaust. Representative material available:

	Commemoration Efforts
	   Jewish Labor and the Holocaust
	   Children of Survivors
	   Holocaust and Genocide Curriculum
	   The Music of the Holocaust
	   What Is Fascism?
	   Triangles and Tribulations: The Politics of Nazi Symbols
	   The Truth about Anne Frank, a 12-class lesson plan
	   Holocaust Denial and The Big Lie
	   The Holocaust—A Guide for Teachers

	[Michael Declan Dunn and Joey Korn, Alliance for a Better Earth]
	The Hornet
Comment	http://www.sas.upenn.edu:80/African_Studies/Hornet/menu_Hornet.html
	The Hornet, based in Ethiopia, is a free computer networking service which promotes the exchange of information about the Horn of Africa. Academics, diplomats, governments, and UN agencies are involved in this information exchange. Samples of documents available:

	Awdal "Republic": Declaration of Independence, [Somalia]
	   Connectivity in Africa, 1996
	   Everything about Qat/khat/kat
	   Horn of Africa Bulletin
	   Horn of Africa Internet Resources Guide
	   Inter Africa Group: "Famine in Ethiopia"
	   Military Intervention in Africa
	   NomadNet
	   South Sudan: A History of Political Domination—A Case of Self-Determination

	[Pan African Development Information System of the UN Economic Commission for Africa]

Comment	**Horus' Web Links to History Resources** http://www.ucr.edu/h-gig/horuslinks.html A good starting place for jumping to virtually any history-related Web site. Over 1,700 Web links are indexed by era, country, and by topic. [Department of History, University of California, Riverside]
Comment	**Images from History** http://library.ccsu.ctstateu.edu/~history/world_history/image_archive/index.html This collection of images related to ancient history includes mostly slides of museum artifacts. [Haines Brown]
Comment	**International Museum of Surgical Science** http://www.imss.org/ The main online feature of this site is the Interactive Antique Illness simulation, in which the user becomes a rural resident in the United States of the 1800s. Through interactive decision making, a cure may be found or the patient may be lost. In Cyber-life, if the first decision doesn't work out, the effects are not permanent—you may try again! Links to other sites concerned with medical history are provided. [The International College of Surgeons]
Comment	**Introduction to the World of Anthropology** http://www.ed.uiuc.edu/students/b-sklar/basic387.html How do anthropologists determine the diets of ancient homonids? This basic tutorial on anthropology gives a glimpse of their research techniques. After learning the basic techniques and concepts, students can complete an excellent simulation, "Now You Can Be an Anthropologist," requiring them to interpret the map of an archeological excavation and draw conclusions about its original inhabitants. [Bonnie Faith Sklar, University of Illinois at Urbana-Champaign]

Comment	Iran/Persia
	http://www.ed.ac.uk/~bhm/iran-history.html
	A thorough historical account explores the history of Persia and Iran from the prehistoric era to the present. Specific sections elaborate on the art, culture, geopolitics, history, geography, literature, and religions of the region.
	[Encyclopedia Britannica]
Comment	Irish Famine
	http://www.emory.edu/FAMINE/
	Illustrated with many beautiful engravings, this unique collection features contemporary accounts of the famed Irish "Potato Famine." A variety of poignant articles are featured from several English and Irish publications of the 1840s, including *The Illustrated London News*, *The Cork Examiner*, *The Pictorial Times*, *Punch*, and *Oxford to Skibbereen*. This exhibit provides outstanding material for covering an event often overlooked in high school world history classes.
	[Steve Taylor]
Comment	Land of Genghis Khan
	http://www.nationalgeographic.com/modules/genghis/index.html
	Help your students explore the life and times of Genghis Khan through this *National Geographic*-sponsored trek through modern Mongolia. This superb online version of the December 1996/February 1997 magazine provides splendid photographs and maps. Excellent age-appropriate lesson plans are available online to augment the beautiful Web pages. If a RealAudio plug-in is available, sound clips can be played to embellish some parts of the story.
	[National Geographic Society]
Comment	Leonardo da Vinci Museum
	http://cellini.leonardo.net/museum/gallery.html#start
	Leonardo da Vinci, accomplished scientist, painter, designer, and futurist, came to epitomize the "Renaissance Man." This electronic museum exhibit honors the man and his many accomplishments and depicts a selected sampling of his

A+

A+

work, featuring his noted paintings "Mona Lisa" and "The Last Supper," futuristic flying machines and weapons, and marvelously detailed sketches and drawings. Some exhibits are a bit short on descriptive text, but the wonderful images of da Vinci's work make it a site worth visiting.

[Jim Pickrell, Leonardo Internet]

Life of Industrial Workers in 19th-Century England

Comment

http://ab.edu/~delcol_l/worker.html

The grim life of nineteenth-century English industrial workers is depicted, often in their own words. One poignant example from eight-year-old Sarah Gooder:
"I'm a trapper in the Gawber pit. It does not tire me, but I have to trap without a light and I'm scared. I go at four and sometimes half past three in the morning, and come out at five and half past. I never go to sleep. Sometimes I sing when I've light, but not in the dark; I dare not sing then. I don't like being in the pit. I am very sleepy when I go sometimes in the morning."

[Reprinted in an old history textbook, *Readings in European History Since 1814*, Jonathan F. Scott and Alexander Baltzly, editors, Appleton-Century-Crofts, Inc., 1930.]

Marxism

Comment

http://www.anu.edu.au/polsci/marx/

This resource focuses upon Karl Marx and his political and economic theories. The *Communist Manifesto* and other Marxist documents are available online. Download an interesting set of graphics pertaining to the rise of communism, including photographs of key players, such as Lenin and Trotsky.

[Rick Kuhn]

Medieval/Renaissance Food

Comment

http://www.pbm.com/~lindahl/food.html

Give your students a taste of aebleskiver, only one of many medieval era recipes to be found through this fun and fascinating archive. Many valuable lessons could involve students in preparing and tasting foods from this historical period. They will be challenged with a different set of weights and measures, the lack of refrigeration, and sometimes unusual ingredients.

[Greg Lindahl]

$A+$

Comment	**Medieval Sourcebook**

http://www.fordham.edu/halsall/sbook.html

A paperback edition of this immense resource on medieval history would be quite expensive and would probably be a multivolume set. Constructed predominantly from public domain and copy-permitted texts, the creator has provided a service of great value to world history teachers of all levels. Most of the documents can be downloaded and copied for classroom use. This virtual archive is overflowing with excellent content. Just a few of the gems to be found among the hundreds of links available through this site:

> The Nicene Creed
> Fief Ceremonies, 12th Century
> Southampton Guild Merchant: Rules
> Gregory VII: Call for a "Crusade," 1174
> Beowulf
> Laws of William the Conqueror
> The Doomsday Book 1086
> Ordinance of Laborers, 1349
> Magna Carta
> Bernard Gui: Inquisitor's Manual (1307-1323)
> Joan of Arc: Letter to the King of England, 1429
> Witchcraft Documents
> Council Legislation on Marriage
> Martin Luther: 95 Theses, 1517
> Marco Polo: On the Tartars (1254-1324)
> Christopher Columbus: Selections from Journal, 1492
> Christopher Columbus: Letter to King and Queen of Spain, probably 1494

[Paul Halsall, Fordham University]

Comment	**Money**

http://www.ex.ac.uk/~RDavies/arian/llyfr.html

At some point in history, eggs, gongs, jade, kettles, leather, amber, beads, nails, pigs, ivory, salt, rice, and wampum have all served as money. This site explores the history of money from ancient civilizations to modern times.

[Glyn and Roy Davies with excerpts from Davies, Glyn. A History of Money from Ancient Times to the Present Day, rev. ed. Cardiff: University of Wales Press, 1996.]

$A+$

Comment	**Napoleon Series**

http://www.ping.be/napoleon.series/

A Sergeant-Major in the Belgian Army has created a beautifully designed, electronic magazine focusing on Napoleon and his era. The great graphics, original articles, frequently updated link list, and "Napoleonic Discussion Forum" make this a first-rate resource. Be sure to take the "Guided Tour on the Waterloo Battlefield." The coverage of Napoleon does not appear devotional, but even-handed. This project is truly a labor of love.

[A. Libert]

A+

Comment

Notable Citizens of the Planet

http://www.tiac.net/users/parallax/

Search the "Biographical Dictionary" for accounts of 18,000 notable men and women from antiquity to the present day. Test your knowledge of historic figures with the "Master Biographer Challenge" interactive quiz. An "Ideas for Students and Teachers" section posts instructional activities applying content from the "Biographical Dictionary."

[The Parallax Group]

Comment

Nuremberg Trials

http://www.courttv.com/casefiles/nuremberg/

In 1945, twenty-one Nazi defendants were tried in Nuremberg for war crimes committed during World War II. The story of these historic trials is told through interviews, actual trial transcripts, and brief biographies of the major participants. An essay examines the definition of war crimes and the impact of this trial on international law.

[Court TV]

Comment

Origins of Humankind

http://www.dealsonline.com/origins/

Devoted to looking objectively at the research and theories related to the origin of the humankind. Each month articles are added to this collection. Sample items:

America's Oldest Mummy
Oldest Stone Tools Found
DNA Links Teacher to 9,000-Year-Old Skeleton

[Human Origins Internet Taskforce]

Comment	## Paris: Urban Sanitation Before the 20th Century
	http://www.op.net/~uarts/krupa/
	It is easy to take the modern sewer systems and water utilities for granted. This intriguing, well-researched site features vivid text and splendid graphics to describe the state of sanitation in the city of Paris prior to the 1900s. Excellent content.
	[Frederique Krupa, University of the Arts, Philadelphia]
Comment	## Penny Magazine
	http://www.history.rochester.edu/pennymag/
	Excerpts from the 1832-1835 editions of the popular nineteenth-century magazine provide a valuable glimpse of everyday life among the English working class.
	"Bring they [sic] children up in learning and obedience, yet without outward austerity. Praise them openly, reprehend them secretly. Give them good countenance, and convenient maintenance, according to they ability, otherwise they life will seem their bondage, and what portion thou shalt leave them at they death they will thank death for it and not thee."
	"Lord Burghley's Advice to His Son Concerning the Treatment of Children," *The Penny Magazine*, No. 215, Aug. 8, 1835.
	[Roger Corrie]
Comment	## Rabbit in the Moon: Mayan Hieroglyphic Writing
	http://www.halfmoon.org/
	Discover why Mayans bound the head of their newborn infants between two boards. Learn to write your name in Mayan hieroglyphics, browse an intriguing collection of logographs, try your hand at translating some hieroglyphic writing, or marvel at the sophistication of the Mayan calendar. Be sure to seek the creator's permission before using any of the items from this site. It is worth the effort, though; this is a winner.
	[Nancy McNelly]

A+

Comment	**Reeder's Egypt Page** http://www.egyptology.com/reeder/ Take a virtual tour of the fascinating tomb of Egyptian King Niusere or browse the beautiful Egyptian Gallery of paintings and photographs. Discover the mysterious Muu and the dance they perform. This charming repository includes numerous links dedicated to the art, archaeology, and history of Ancient Egypt. [Greg Reeder, KMT Communications]
Comment	**Retanet** http://ladb.unm.edu/retanet/plans/ This high school Latin America lesson plan exchange currently features 65 teacher-made social studies lessons. A few samples: Using Cartagrams to Learn about Latin America Human Rights in Latin America: The Death Squads Mexican Stereotypes: True or False? Urbanization in the Amazon Basin: Can Indigenous People Survive? Migration and Immigration Borders: A Multi-Dimensional Approach Culture—Do I Have That? [Latin America Data Base (LADB), Latin American Institute, University of New Mexico]
Comment	**Roman Law** http://www.abdn.ac.uk/~law113/rl/text/text.htm Most history teachers have heard of the Romans' Twelve Tables or the Code of Hammurabi, but few have actually seen them. View full-text translations of these primary documents, plus a number of related scholarly works at this useful archive. [E. Metzger, University of Aberdeen]
Comment	**Romarch: Roman Art and Archaeology** http://www-personal.umich.edu/~pfoss/ROMARCH.html If you love things Roman, you will delight in this immense depository of information on the art and archaeology of Italy

and the Roman provinces (ca. 1000 BC-AD 700). Though these areas are the primary focus, much of interest can be found on Roman law, society, culture, war, and religion. The authors have screened potential sites to include only those of the highest academic quality. The enormous body of content linked here would be overwhelming if it were not so well organized.

[Dr. Pedar W. Foss & Sean O'Neill, Department of Classics, University of Cincinnati and the Interdepartmental Program in Classical Art and Archaeology at the University of Michigan]

Comment	### Rome Project http://www.dalton.org/groups/rome/ Another huge collection of resources on ancient Rome, organized into several categories: literature, archaeology, military, political, drama, religion, philosophy, and maps. [Dr. Neil Goldberg, The Dalton School]
Comment	### Rome Reborn: The Vatican Library & Renaissance Culture http://sunsite.unc.edu/expo/vatican.exhibit/exhibit/Main_Hall.html An online display of the Library of Congress exhibition of 200 of the Vatican Library's most precious manuscripts, books, and maps, detailing the emergence of Rome as a political and scholarly tour de force during the Renaissance. The exhibit is composed of nine sections: The Vatican Library; Archaeology; Humanism; Mathematics; Music; Medicine & Biology; Nature Described; A Wider World I: How the Orient Came to Rome; and A Wider World II: How Rome Went to China. Brief text descriptions and beautiful online images depicting the most cherished documents from the Vatican's collection portray the influence of the Vatican Library in this cultural and political transformation. [Library of Congress]
Comment	### Russian Constitution http://www.bucknell.edu/departments/russian/const/constit.html

Following the dissolution of the U.S.S.R., the Constitution of the Russian Federation was ratified on December 12, 1993. A full English text translation is provided.

[Russian Department, Bucknell University]

Comment

Searching for China

http://www.kn.pacbell.com/wired/China/ChinaQuest.html

Students, playing roles as members of a fact-finding team (i.e., foreign investor, human rights activist, etc.) to China, investigate a variety of resources to arrive at policy conclusions and submit an action plan to the U.S. government. A very sophisticated simulation develops a number of basic learning skills in participating students and conveys the complexity of forming a policy toward China. It includes an extensive dossier of background material representing the various economic, political, social, religious, and cultural interests affecting life in China and its relationship with the rest of the world. This is truly an outstanding active learning experience.

[Pacific Bell]

Comment

Secrets of the Norman Invasion

http://www.cablenet.net/pages/book/index.htm

A rather academic treatise on the location of the Battle of Hastings, this site provides much background information on the invasion including related archaeological investigations.

[Nick Austin]

Comment

Seven Wonders of the Ancient World

http://pharos.bu.edu/Egypt/Wonders/

How many of the Seven Wonders of the Ancient World can you name? Which one of the seven survives today? Each is not only named, but delightfully described and illustrated in this pleasantly designed Cyber-guide. A map indicates the location of each of these remarkable structures. Fifteen additional long-forgotten wonders are also included in the collection, as well as fifteen wonders of the modern world and thirteen natural wonders.

[Alaa K. Ashmawy]

Comment	### Smithsonian: American Treasure House for Learning
	http://www.si.edu/newstart.htm
	The online version of "America's attic" offers a wide spectrum of educational exhibits and resources. Rummage the extensive collection of Americana, which includes many interest-arousing gems (including the Hope Diamond).
	[The Smithsonian Institution]
Comment	### Soviet Archive Document
	http://sunsite.unc.edu/pjones/russian/outline.html
	Download sample pages from the Russian archive documents now housed in the Library of Congress. Read translations of previously secret memos and letters by Russian leaders discussing the secret police, anti-religion campaigns, the Cuban Missile Crisis, attacks on the intelligentsia, and the nuclear disaster at Chernobyl.
	[Library of Congress]
Comment	### Tale of the Airplane
	http://hawaii.cogsci.uiuc.edu/invent/taleplane.html
	This enthusiastic, multimedia account of the evolution of the airplane contains well-researched, clearly written text, and splendid historical photographs and illustrations While the account is probably over kill for world history classes, avid aviation fans (students or otherwise) will relish this site. Head students here if they have Internet access. Teachers can devise some interesting history lessons from its mass of content.
	[Gary Bradshaw]
Comment	### Victoria and Albert, Vicky & The Kaiser
	http://www.dhm.de/ENGLISH/ausstellungen/victalb/
	This splendid online version of a 1997 German Historical Museum exhibit depicts the history of Anglo-German relations during the reign of Queen Victoria. The queen, herself of German descent, married Albert of Saxe-Coburg and Gotha. Six of their nine children married German spouses. Their oldest daughter Vicky, by marrying the Crown Prince of Prussia, became a German Empress. Hence, there was a

strong lifelong interrelationship between the reign of Victoria and the evolution of Germany. This connection is beautifully told through this virtual tour of the museum's exhibit.

[German Historical Museum]

A+

Victorian Era

Comment

http://www.stg.brown.edu/projects/hypertext/landow/victorian/victov.html

The Victorian Era encompasses a variety of cultural, political, architectural, literary, and scientific events which occurred during the reign of Queen Victoria (1837-1901). Dr. Landow, his colleagues, and his students have assembled an impressive array of original resources and links related to this important period. The coverage of English literature is particularly strong; the site is a sterling reference for students and scholars interested in this period of British development.

[George P. Landow, Professor of English and Art History, Brown University]

A+

United Nations CyberSchoolBus

Comment

http://www.un.org/Pubs/CyberSchoolBus/main.htm

Great lessons related to the United Nations and world issues are collected in this elegant, professionally done treasury. Excellent lesson plans and student activities, geared for all grade levels, are stored here. Information on the renowned Model United Nations simulation are included.

[United Nations Publications]

Web Museum of Latin America

Comment

http://museos.web.com.mx/

A cutting edge concept, this is an online master collection of Latin American museum Web pages. The Museum of the Federal Territory Amazonas is particularly recommended for its well-researched exhibits and vivid online photographs and illustrations. An online tour of these museums is the next best thing to being there. Seldom will such in-depth and rich coverage be given to most of the topics in any North American museum. One important tip: to switch from Spanish to the English version after you have made your selection, click on the illustration of lips at the bottom of the screen.

[A. Zepeda, A. Bejar, K. R. Durand, E. Llaguno, I. Cervantes, J. L. Bravo, J. F. Puente]

World History Compass

Comment

http://www.lexiconn.com/lis/schcomp/whl/whlindex.htm

Nothing fancy here, just an impressive jumplist of helpful resources on world and United States history, categorized by country.

[Schiller Computing]

World History to 1500

Comment

http://www.byuh.edu/coursework/hist201/

This hyperlink, virtual library offers links to dozens of interesting and informative world history resources, everything from an overview of Zoroastrianism to weapons of the Stone Age. The easily navigable categories include not only Euro-American history, but also outstanding resources on the early history and culture of Africa, China, India, and other world regions.

[Orson Ka'ili, Brigham Young University—Hawaii]

World of the Vikings

Comment

http://www.demon.co.uk/past/vikings/

This link-reliant clearinghouse for all things related to Vikings is a true bonanza for world history teachers. Major sections of academic material feature Norse mythology, heritage, Viking expeditions, and Nordic peoples.

[Past Forward Limited]

World War II Propaganda Posters

Comment

http://www.openstore.com/posters/

Twenty-six patriotic World War II propaganda posters commissioned by various agencies of the U.S. government are available as colorful JPEG images.

[J. D. Ross]

Comment	**World's Columbian Exposition** http://xroads.virginia.edu/~MA96/WCE/title.html Tour this electronic exhibit of the popular 1893 World Columbian Exposition, the international fair that introduced the Ferris wheel and the ice-cream cone. Beyond providing a charming, yet well-documented and scholarly glimpse of the culture and technology of the Gay Nineties, this hypertext exhibit does a beautiful job of assessing the legacy of the fair and the preview it provided of the twentieth century. [Julie K. Rose]

ELECTRONIC MAILING LISTS: WORLD HISTORY

Many electronic mailing lists (or discussion groups) focus on topics of interest to world history teachers and students. It is easy to subscribe. For example, to subscribe to the mailing list on African history:

Send an e-mail message to: LISTSERV@MSU.EDU

Usually it is best to leave the "Subject" line blank. If your e-mail software requires something in the subject line, simply type a period.

Enter the message: subscribe H-AFRICA John Doe

Remember to enter your name instead of John Doe.

The format for the message is: subscribe <List_Name> <Your_Full_Name>

Aia
Archaeology forum
E-mail to: LISTSERV@CC.BRYNMAWR.EDU

Ancien-L
Ancient history of the Mediterranean region
E-mail to: LISTSERV@ULKYVM.BITNET

ANE
Ancient Near East
E-mail to: MAJORDOMO@OI.UCHICAGO.EDU

Celtic-L
Celtic history and culture
E-mail to: LISTSERV@IRLEARN.UCD.IE

Ecchst-L
Church history
E-mail to: LISTSERV@BGU.EDU

EEJH
Eastern European Jewish history and culture
E-mail to: MAJORDOMO@ORT.ORG

Emedch-L
History of medieval China
E-mail to: LISTSERV@USCVM

Emhist-L
Early modern history
E-mail to: LISTSERV@RUTVM1.RUTGERS.EDU

H-Africa
African history forum
E-mail to: LISTSERV@MSU.EDU

H-Albion
Forum on British and Irish history
E-mail to: LISTSERV@UICVM.UIC.EDU

H-Antis
History of anti-Semitism
E-mail to: LISTSERV@MSU.EDU

H-Asia
History of Asia
E-mail to: LISTSERV@LIST.SERV.UIC.EDU

H-Ideas
History of ideas
E-mail to: LISTSERV@UICVM.UIC.EDU

H-Latam
History of Latin America
E-mail to: LISTSERV@UICVM.UIC.EDU

H-Law
Legal history
E-mail to: LISTSERV@UICVM.UIC.EDU

H-Pol
Political history
E-mail to: LISTSERV@UICVM.UIC.EDU

H-World
Teaching world history
E-mail to: LISTSERV@MSU.EDU

History
Assorted discussions on history
E-mail to: LISTSERV@RUTVM1.RUTGERS.EDU

Ioudaios-L
Jewish history and culture
E-mail to: LISTSERV@LEHIGH.EDU

Islam-L
History of Islamic religion and culture
E-mail to: LISTSERV@ULKYVM.BITNET

Labor-L
Western hemisphere labor history and issues
E-mail to: LISTSERV@YORKVM1.BITNET

Mediev-L
Medieval history forum
E-mail to: LISTSERV@UKANVM.CC.UKANS.EDU

Milhst-L
Military history
E-mail to: LISTSERV@UKANVM.CC.UKANS.EDU

Modelun
Model U.N. newsletter
E-mail to: LISTSERV@INDYCMS.IUPUI.EDU

Nat-1492
Discussion of Columbus' voyage and its impact
E-mail to: LISTSERV@TAVM1.BITNET

Persia-L
Persian history
E-mail to: LISTSERV@EMUVM1.CC.EMORY.EDU

Renais-L
Renaissance history forum
E-mail to: LISTSERV@ULKYVM.LOUISVILLE.EDU

Romearch
Roman archaeology
E-mail to: MAJORDOMO@ROME.CLASSICS.LSU.UMICH.EDU

Rushist

Russian history discussion
E-mail to: LISTSERV@CSEARN.BITNET

Sovhist

History of the Soviet Union 1917-1991
E-mail to: LISTSERV@VM.USC.EDU

Vwar-L

Vietnam war forum
E-mail to: LISTSERV@UBVM.BITNET

Victoria

The Victorian Era in Britain
E-mail to: LISTSERV@IUBVM.EDU

World-L

Discussion of history from a non-Eurocentric perspective
E-mail to: LISTSERV@UBVM.CC.BUFFALO.EDU

WWI-L

History of the First World War
E-mail to: LISTSERV@UKANAIX.CC.UKAN.EDU

WWII-L

World War II forum
E-mail to: LISTSERV@UBVM.CC.BUFFALO.EDU

Newsgroups: World History

alt.history.ocean-liners.titanic	Folks real interested in the Titanic
alt.legend.king-arthur	Legends of King Arthur
rec.aviation.military	Military aircraft
rec.food.historic	History of food preparation; ancient recipes
sci.classics	Study of classical literature, art, history
soc.culture.african	African culture
soc.culture.african.american	African-American culture
soc.culture.china	Chinese culture
soc.culture.french	French history and culture

Newsgroups: World History (Continued)

soc.culture.german	German history and culture
soc.culture.jewish.holocaust	Effects of the Holocaust
soc.culture.native	Aboriginal people anywhere
soc.culture.scottish	Culture and history of Scotland
soc.culture.spain	Spanish culture and events
soc.culture.usa	Culture of the U.S.
soc.genealogy.african	Tracing ancestors from Africa
soc.history	General discusion about history
soc.history.african	African history
soc.history.ancient	History of ancient civilizations
soc.history.living	Living history hobbyists' forum
soc.history.medieval	Medieval/renaissance times
soc.history.moderated	Moderated history discussion group
soc.history.science	Historical science discussions
soc.history.war.misc	General discussions of wars of the past
soc.history.what-if	Wild conjecture on different historical endings

Section 5

CONSUMER ECONOMICS

BEST WEB SITES: CONSUMER ECONOMICS

Comment	**101 Uses for Your Old Shoes 'n other Stuff** http://www.knosso.com/Shoes/index.html What do you do with grandpa's eyeglasses or old golf clubs? For creative ideas on decluttering your home of cast-offs, white elephants, and unwanted inheritances, consult the electronic edition of *101 Ways to Reuse Your Old Shoes 'n Other Stuff: A Money-Saving Guide to Reusing, Repairing, and Renting Goods in the Lower Mainland.* A good source for recycling project ideas. [Greater Vancouver Regional District Solid Waste Department]
Comment	**Advertising** http://www.arcade.uiowa.edu/gw/comm/advertising.html Access dozens of links to Web pages dealing with all aspects of advertising. Several particularly interesting ones relate to its history. [University of Iowa Library]
Comment	**American Express University** http://www.americanexpress.com/student/club/club.html One of the best commercial sites, filled with eye-catching graphics and valuable information on helping young people manage their money wisely. Sample topics: budgeting, getting a job, financing college. [American Express]
Comment	**Better Business Bureau** http://www.bbb.org/ Better Business Bureaus provide important information and services to both consumers and businesses. Their Web site includes a resource library of BBB consumer buying guides, scam alerts, information on ethical advertising and selling practices, and a directory of all 137 local BBB offices with hot links to those with Web pages. Users can also file consumer complaints online. [Council of Better Business Bureaus]

Comment	**Biztools** http://www.cybersolve.com/tools1.html Students are introduced to three basic business tools: The Financial Calculator figures the growth of an investment at different points in time using a variety of cash flow assumptions. This calculator is useful for determining the length of a mortgage, the changing value of an investment, or the amount needed to create a desired retirement income. Very user friendly, with clear directions. Breakeven Analysis calculates the level of sales required for a business to break even. It could be used to figure the volume of sales needed to break even, obtain a desired profit, or determine the price to be charged for a product or service. A good tool for giving students insight into business decision making. Ratio Analysis transforms accounting numbers taken from a financial statement into meaningful ratios that reveal the strengths and weaknesses of a business. A more advanced instrument, but it should prove valuable in analyzing financial trends and results of a hypothetical or real business. Excellent tutorials guide students through each of the three business tools. Teachers can design some splendid lessons around this site if their students have direct access to the Internet. [Cybersolve]
Comment	**Bureau of Labor Statistics** http://stats.bls.gov:80/datahome.htm Download a wide array of employment and wage statistics from this government site. The "Economy at a Glance" page and recent news releases provide much more current data than likely found in any textbook or journal article. [U.S. Department of Labor]
Comment	**Business Week Online** http://www.businessweek.com/ The electronic edition of America's best-selling business magazine provides current national and international business news. Some pages are a bit slow loading as they are unusually heavy with graphics. [The McGraw-Hill Companies Inc.]

Comment	Canadian National Debt http://www.cam.org/~mdavies/cgi-bin/CanClock.cgi The U.S. isn't the only nation plagued by a rapidly accumulating national debt. Click the debt clock and a few seconds later click it again to discover the huge increases in the debt toll within just a few seconds or minutes. [Max Davies, Open Universal Software]
Comment	CARveat Emptor (Car Buyer Beware) http://www.well.com/user/kr2/ Discover the tricks of shady car sales persons and develop the art of self-defense in auto buying with the help of this practical, no-nonsense Web page. [R. Rand Knox]
Comment	Common Cause http://www.commoncause.org/ This non-profit citizens' advocate group has developed a most informative and professionally designed Web page. Hard-hitting investigative articles probing a range of contemporary issues support the organization's mission of "promoting open, honest and accountable government." Some well-researched, thought-provoking reports on the effects of money in politics can be found here. [Common Cause]
Comment	Consumer Guide http://cg.gte.net/ What is the "Best Buy" in stereo headset radios? What do all those letters mean on a fire extinguisher? What should one look for in buying a used car? The *Consumer Guide* provides online ratings, reviews, and recommendations for a wide range of products. [Publications International, Ltd. and GTE Directories Corp.]
Comment	Consumer Health and Safety http://www.essential.org/cchs/cchs.html

The Coalition for Consumer Health and Safety is a partnership of consumer, health, and insurance groups working together to promote consumer health and safety.

This Web site seeks to educate the public and offer effective solutions in three areas: Transportation Safety, Safety in the Home, and Personal Health and Wellness. Its online brochure, "Hidden Hazards," provides warnings of potential perils which could easily be overlooked (for example, poisoning from improperly cooked foods, mixing alcohol and certain medications, and fat-free desserts). Download the annual report, "The Nation's Health and Safety: A Status Report," which provides an update on such health issues as AIDS, drinking water safety, and tobacco usage.

[The Coalition for Consumer Health and Safety]

Consumer Information Center

Comment

http://www.pueblo.gsa.gov/textver/t_main.htm

Provides online text editions of 200 of the best consumer publications from the federal government. Features include:

> Consumer Resource Handbook
> Consumer Information Catalog (view online or download)
> Consumer News You Can Use
> Special Publications of Consumer Interest
> What Is CIC? Background and Activities

[U.S. General Services Administration]

Consumer Law Page

Comment

http://consumerlawpage.com/

Access over 100 public domain brochures covering law-related topics of interest to consumers. These brochures are from various organizations, including the Federal Trade Commission (FTC), the Environmental Protection Agency (EPA), and the U.S. Department of Commerce. Topic areas include: automobiles, banking, credit, career/employment, health & medical, investing, loans/mortgages, and products & services.

[Alexander Law Firm]

Consumer Price Indexes

Comment

http://stats.bls.gov:80/cpihome.htm

This official government site includes everything you could possibly want to know about consumer price indexes: how they are calculated, uses of the data, effects of inflation, and much more.

[Bureau of Labor Statistics]

Comment

Consumer Product Safety Commission

http://www.cpsc.gov/

Reports on hazardous products (such as lead-based paint on playground equipment) are available from this independent watchdog agency. A master list of defective products under recall is available here.

[U.S. Consumer Product Safety Commission]

Comment

Consumer Product Testing Laboratory for Kids

http://jsd.k12.ak.us/WWW/Projects/menr/4thGrade/ConProd.html

Fourth-grade students conducted product evaluations on three different brands of three different products: watermelon-flavored bubble gum, orange juice, and colored pencils. Using blind, controlled testing procedures the students selected their favorite of each product. Check out their procedures and results in this clever online report.

[Mendenhall River Community School]

Comment

Consumer Rights

http://www.aarp.org/programs/consumer/home.html

The American Association for Retired Persons produces a number of valuable consumer publications that can be accessed online. Not just for older folks, these are brief, well-researched documents covering a variety of consumer-oriented issues.

[American Association for Retired Persons]

Comment

Consumer World

http://www.consumerworld.org/

Colorful, easy-to-use collection of over 1,400 consumer-related Web sites. Major categories: consumer news, governmental agencies, information resources, companies, travel, entertainment, money, and shopping. A must-see site!

[Edgar Dworsky, consumer advocate/educator and attorney]

Comment	### Consumers Corner http://www.usnews.com/usnews/nycu/consume.htm Check out weekly articles on a variety of consumer-related topics. [U.S. News Online]
Comment	### Consumer's Resource Handbook http://www.pueblo.gsa.gov/1997crh/res_pref.pdf Download this popular federal publication free. A most helpful consumer resource, this gem is filled with tips for wise purchasing and listings of resources for resolving consumer disputes. The file is broken into several sections for ease in downloading. [Consumer Services Center]
Comment	### Cost-of-living Comparator http://cgi.pathfinder.com/@@J156dwYAy4xQdG@7/cgi-bin/Money/col.cgi Compare the expenses of living in any two of 500 cities in the United States. [*Money* Online]
Comment	### Credit 101: The Basics of Consumer Credit Reports http://www.experian.com/personal/index.html A basic primer on consumer credit reports: what is in them, how to order them, and how they are used. As the site is maintained by a supplier of credit information services, the information does emphasize the positive aspects of credit reports. [Experian]
Comment	### Currency Exchange and The Gang of Fifteen http://ecedweb.unomaha.edu/gang1.htm Students pursue elusive international criminals by tracking their credit card charges. This fun, yet educationally sound, simulation teaches students to convert various foreign currencies into U.S. dollars. [Eric Enholm, Walnut Jr. High School, Grand Island, NE]

Comment	**Cybercop Precinct House** http://www.ucan.org/ Discover the scams and schemes being perpetrated over the Internet. Proposed legislation for regulating the Internet is also being monitored at this site. [UCAN/Utility Consumers' Action Network]
Comment	**Design Paradise** http://ananke.advanced.org/2111/ Three high school students won the "Best Educational Design" category in the ThinkQuest '96 competition with this online simulation game. It is designed to encourage students to weigh the factors which comprise a stable and prosperous economy. In assuming the role of CEO of a major development company, students consider the needs of industry, environment, and population in attaining their objectives. This project embodies the creative potential of the Internet for excellent classroom instruction. [Jeff Chan of Roosevelt High School; Darren Sueoka and Dawn Sueoka of Moanalua High School, Honolulu, HI]
Comment	**EcEdWeb** http://ecedweb.unomaha.edu/ The Economic Education Web site organizes a variety of instructional resources for economics teachers. It has several very good simulation games. Check out "Using the Internet to Teach Economics: An Idea Page" for examples of how other teachers have incorporated the Information Superhighway into their lesson plans. The site includes information for teachers of all levels, even featuring a few economics lesson ideas for K-4 teachers. [University of Nebraska, Omaha, Center for Economic Education]
Comment	**Economic Statistics Briefing Room** http://www.whitehouse.gov/fsbr/esbr.html This service provides convenient access to current federal economic indicators, providing links to information generat-

ed by several federal agencies. Excellent, easy-to-read charts and graphs summarize economic data in the following categories:

Output
Income
Employment, Unemployment, and Earnings
Production and Business Activity
Prices
Money, Credit, and Securities Markets
Transportation
International Statistics

[The White House]

Comment

Economics Lesson Plans

http://www.digicity.com/lesson/l_econ.htm

A dozen or so K-12 lesson plans for budgeting, stock market investing, charting, borrowing, and saving are included in this Web site.

[The Education Station]

Comment

Economy Track: USA Today

http://www.usatoday.com/money/economy/econ0001.htm

Discover practical, Associated Press/*USA Today* articles and statistics on all aspects of U.S. economic conditions. As they are not overly technical, many of these charts could be incorporated into excellent data analysis lesson plans.

[*USA Today*]

Comment

Edmund's Automobile Buying Guide

http://www.edmunds.com/

Online version of the terrific information-packed automobile buying guide. A great source of information for anything related to purchasing new or used cars or trucks; this is an extensive depository of auto safety information and repair manuals.

[Edmund Publications Corporation]

A+

Comment	**Edustock**
	http://tqd.advanced.org/3088/
	To discover such a beautifully designed, educationally sound, realtime stock simlulation game is a thrill, enhanced by the fact that it was created by three young students. Their design was the Grand Prize winner in the 1996 ThinkQuest competition. Using 20-minute-delayed stock quotes, the simulation and tutorials teach students (and adults) how to select and purchase stocks.
	[Michael Schulman, Derek Goldstein, and Jason Yang, Winston Churchill High School, Potomac, MD]
Comment	**Employment Briefing Room: Economics Statistics**
	http://www.whitehouse.gov/fsbr/employment.html
	A collection of easy-to-read charts and graphs depicting the most current U.S. employment statistics. Updated at least monthly from Bureau of Labor statistics, these data include: Civilian Labor Force, Unemployment, Unemployment Rate, Employees on Nonfarm Payrolls, Average Weekly Hours, Average Hourly Employment Cost, and Productivity.
	[The White House]
Comment	**FDA Consumer**
	http://www.fda.gov/fdahomepage.html
	One of the best sources for current, accurate information on food and prescription drugs, featuring special sections on: medical devices, cosmetics, toxicology, AIDS, cancer, and children and tobacco. An excellent series of articles can be downloaded from the "On the Teen Scene" section, including:
	Acne Agony Cosmetics and Reality Dodging The Rays Eating Disorders Require Medical Attention Enjoy, Protect The Best Ears of Your Life Food Label Makes Good Eating Easier Good News about Good Nutrition Should You Go on A Diet? Using Over-The-Counter Medications Wisely
	[U.S. Food & Drug Administration]

Comment	**Federal Reserve Board** http://www.bog.frb.fed.us/ This is the first place to look for current interest rate statistics, including bank prime rates, U.S. government securities rates, foreign exchange rates, and conventional mortgage rates. Testimony and speeches of Federal Reserve Board members, press releases of board actions, legal interpretations, and reports to Congress provide a spate of instructional material to stimulate student thinking and discussion. [Federal Reserve Board]
Comment	**Federal Trade Commission** http://www.ftc.gov/ Charged with enforcing federal antitrust and consumer protection laws, the F.T.C. works to eliminate unfair or deceptive practices in the marketplace. There are some consumer education gems hidden here. Be sure to check out the "Telemarketing Fraud" and "Consumer Alert" sections for the latest word on scams and rip-offs. [Federal Trade Commission]
	Fortune This exceptionally well-organized, online edition of the prestigious financial publication contains articles on investments, business, and economic trends. A text-only version is available for users without graphics capability. A search engine permits easy searches of archived issues. [Time Warner]
Comment	**Frugal Corner** http://www.best.com/~piner/frugal.html Get more out of life at less cost. The Frugal Corner includes an assortment of sources on frugality and simplicity that encompass not only money, but also "time, drains on your mental, physical, and spiritual energy, general quality of life, and the environment." [Piner]

Comment	*Global Grocery List* http://www.landmark-project.com/ggl.html Students compare local prices of fifteen specific food items with those submitted by students from around the world. Suggestions to teachers for follow-up lessons are included. New data are collected each year. [David Warlick]

Comment	*Good Housekeeping Institute*
	
	http://homearts.com/gh/toc/osinstit.htm
	
	Which steering wheel locks provide the best protection? Is it a waste of money to buy premium gasoline? This helpful database provides answers to these and hundreds of other consumer questions. Read monthly articles or search a massive archive of articles from the following magazines:
	
	    Good Housekeeping
	    Popular Mechanics
	    Country Living
	    Redbook
	
	[The Hearst Corporation]

Comment	*Homebuyer's Fair* http://www.homefair.com/home/ A thorough resource on homebuying. Useful tools can be found in the "Popular Exhibits" section, including: The Salary Calculator, The Moving Calculator, Intelligent Mortgage Agent, and Mortgage Qualification Calculator. Additional features include: Mortgage Finance Resources, First Time Buyer Info, Buying a Home, Relocation Information, and Apartments. [Arnold Kling, Homebuyer's Fair]
Comment	*Ideas to Help Your Money Do More* http://www.centura.com/articles/arthome.html Articles on common banking-related consumer questions are assembled in this bank-sponsored Web site. A glossary of banking and investment terms is also included. Among recent topics are:

Five Smart Moves in Retirement Planning
CDs with Muscle: A Strong Alternative for Your Savings
The Factors Affecting the Price of A Home
Debit Cards: Paperless Checks That Are Worth Checking Out
Get A Grip! Letting Go of Financial Worries
How Much Does It Cost to Raise A Child?

[North Carolina's Centura Banks]

Comment

Insurance News Network

http://www.insure.com/

For most adults, purchasing insurance represents a murky financial mystery, absorbing thousands of dollars and countless hours. This guide to auto, home, and life insurance is a great resource for making objective benchmark comparisons among companies. It includes statistics on auto-theft rates. The home insurance section clarifies the different types of coverage in a homeowner's policy (HO-1 through HO-6) and state-by-state price comparisons.

[Philip Moeller, financial journalist and designer of digitized information services]

Comment

Investing for Kids

http://tqd.advanced.org/3096/

A+

Designed by three students, this colorful, informative introduction to investing and saving embodies the great potential of the Web as a learning and teaching tool. Three levels of instruction provide ample teaching content for teachers of all grade levels. Adults would also find this site worth exploring. "The Stock Portfolio Game" is a superb online investment simulation, teaching students how to select, purchase, monitor, and sell stocks. These young men have made a first-rate contribution to Cyberspace instruction.

[David Leung, Steven Ngai, & Hassan Mirza; Palos Verdes (CA) Peninsula High School students]

Comment

Kiplinger's Personal Finance Magazine

http://www.kiplinger.com/magazine/departme.html

The online edition of the authoritative financial advisory journal includes an archive of past issues, valuable feature articles, as well as numerous items in each of the following monthly departments:

The Months Ahead
Saving & Investing
Managing Your Money
Spending
My Personal Finances

[The Kiplinger Washington Editors]

Comment

Lemon Car Page

http://www.mindspring.com/~wf1/

What recourse is available to the buyer of a car that turns out to be a lemon? What protection do state "Lemon Laws" have to offer? Practical advice and useful information are provided here.

[Law office of T. Michael Flinn]

Comment

Look Who's Footing the Bill

http://www.kn.pacbell.com/wired/democracy/debtquest.html

This thought-provoking simulation invites students to grapple with the issue of balancing the U.S. national budget. After working through the "Balance the Budget Game," student teams draft letters to their Congressional representatives and senators presenting their case on how the budget should be allocated. A good start toward creating informed citizens of tomorrow.

[Education First Fellows]

Comment

National Budget Simulation

http://garnet.berkeley.edu:3333/budget/budget-1.html

This simple simulation forces students to wrestle with the trade-offs policy makers must make to balance the budget. In this online simulation students cut the federal fiscal deficit to achieve a balanced budget. They must decide which items must be cut and which should receive increased spending. Both a long and short version are available. The site also includes links to other sites related to the national budget.

[UC-Berkeley's Center for Community Economic Research]

Comment

National Consumer Fraud Information Center

http://www.fraud.org/

This independent organization, founded to help people report fraud and avoid becoming victims, provides daily online fraud alerts. A specific emphasis on telemarketing scams and Internet fraud has developed.

[National Consumers League]

	National Debt Clock
Comment	http://www.brillig.com:80/debt_clock/

Obtain up-to-the-minute information on the amount of the growing United States national debt. A variety of creative activities could be generated from this rapidly changing benchmark. Have students graph the increase over several days. Translate those amounts into buying power—for example, the number of school computers or bicycles that could be bought each day with that amount of money. It is an astonishing number just to write on the board.

[Ed Hall]

National Food Safety Database

Comment

http://www.agen.ufl.edu/~foodsaf/foodsaf.html

Obtain scientifically sound information on the safe handling of food at home or in industry. A wide assortment of information is available here, either online or as Adobe Acrobat files. A small sampling of the pickings:

> General Food Safety Information
> Foodborne Contaminants
> Food Safety Outside the Home
> Holiday Food Safety
> USDA/FDA Food Illness Education Information Center Database
> North Carolina State University's Notebook of Food and Food Safety Information
> Handling Wild Game Meat Safely
> Nutrition Information
> Food Residues and Ingredients
> Biotechnology and Food
> Seafood Safety

[University of Florida; U.S. Department of Agriculture]

National Highway Traffic Safety Administration

Comment

http://www.nhtsa.dot.gov/

NHTSA is charged with reducing injuries, deaths, and economic losses incurred in motor vehicle accidents. Some of the featured resources in their site:

> Vehicle and Equipment Information
> Safety Problems & Issues
> Office of Defects Investigation—Recall Database
> Regulations & Standards
> Crash Information
> Traffic Safety Facts
> Injury Prevention
> Airbags, Child Safety Seats, & Restraint Systems
> Alcohol & Drugs
> Traffic Safety Digest
> Highway Safety Programs: Campaign Safe & Sober
> State Legislative Fact Sheets

[U.S. Department of Transportation]

National Institute on Aging Information Center

Comment

http://www.nih.gov/nia/health/pubpub/pubpub.htm

Download authoritative educational materials on various topics pertaining to health and aging. Sample fare:

> Crime and the Elderly
> Health Quackery
> Medicines: Use Them Safely
> Shots for Safety
> What to Do about the Flu

[The National Institute on Aging, National Institutes of Health]

National Institute for Consumer Education

Comment

http://www.emich.edu/public/coe/nice/nice.html

A must-see site for the consumer economics teacher. Filled with valuable teaching resources, lesson plans, legislative updates, and links to other useful resources. A partial listing:

> Mini-Lessons
> > Auto Leasing
> > College Financial Aid
> > College Student Budget
> > Comparison Shopping
> > Credit Issues: Women and Divorce
> > How to Choose A Credit Card
> > How to Complain
> > Saving for A College Education
> > Students and Credit Cards

Resource Lists
Advertising and Young Consumers
Fraud on The Internet
Micro-Society—Elementary
Money Management Youth
Personal Finance
Consumer Economics Textbooks

Selected Full-Text Resources
Benefits of Consumer Education
Consumer Education for High School Students
Consumer Education for the Elementary School
66 Ways to Save Money

[College of Education, Eastern Michigan University]

Online Money

Comment

http://pathfinder.com/money/

Superb resource on managing money. A partial listing:

Marketwatch, providing current market figures
Quick Quotes provides 15-minute-delayed stock quotes
Mortgage calculator computes, "How much house can you afford?"
Money's annual college guide
Career skills test
Numerous feature articles on all aspects of money management

[*Money*, personal finance magazine]

Our Money

Comment

http://woodrow.mpls.frb.fed.us/econed/curric/money.html

Four captivating mini-lessons are presented: Face of U.S. Currency, Counterfeit Protection, 1996 Currency Redesign, The History of Money. A teacher's guide and review questions are included.

[Federal Reserve Bank of Minneapolis]

Personal Portfolio

Comment

http://www.irnet.com/pages/gatelogin.stm

Enter a list of stocks and automatically check prices of your personal portfolio daily. Also access information about companies and market news items.

[*San Francisco Chronicle*]

Comment	**Privacy Rights Clearinghouse**
	
	http://www.privacyrights.org/
	
	Dedicated to the protection of personal privacy, this unique site offers valuable information and practical suggestions on safeguarding individual privacy. Teachers have permission to download these outstanding educational fact sheets for use in classes:
	
	    Privacy Survival Guide
	    Wireless Communications: Cordless/Cellular Phones and
	    Pagers
	    How to Put an End to Harassing Phone Calls
	    Junk Mail: How Did They All Get My Address?
	    Telemarketing: Whatever Happened to a Quiet Evening at
	    Home?
	    How Private Is My Credit Report?
	    Employee Monitoring: Is There Privacy in the Workplace?
	    How Private Is My Medical Information?
	    Wiretapping and Eavesdropping: Is There Cause for
	    Concern?
	    From Cradle to Grave: Government Records and Your
	    Privacy
	    A Checklist of Responsible Information-Handling Practices
	    Paying by Credit Card or Check: What Can Merchants Ask?
	    Employment Background Checks: A Jobseeker's Guide
	    Coping with Identity Theft: What to Do When an Impostor
	    Strikes
	    Privacy in Cyberspace: Rules of the Road for the
	    Information Superhighway
	    Caller ID and My Privacy: What Do I Need to Know?
	
	Spanish editions are also available.
	
	[Utility Consumers' Action Network (UCAN)]

Comment	**Product Review Net** http://www.productreviewnet.com/ Enter the name of a product to search hundreds of Internet resources to obtain articles making product comparisons. [Rain Corporation]
Comment	**Public Debt** http://www.publicdebt.treas.gov/ Anything and everything about the U.S. federal debt is included in this comprehensive Web page. Major topics include:

The Public Debt of the U.S., to the penny...
Historical Debt
Interest Expense on the Public Debt Outstanding
Frequently Asked Questions

[United States Department of Treasury]

Securities and Exchange Commission

Comment

http://www.sec.gov/

Access EDGAR, the "Electronic Data Gathering, Analysis, and Retrieval" system, for retrieving forms submitted by companies to the U.S. Securities and Exchange Commission (SEC). The site also includes information on investor complaints, SEC rules, and enforcement actions.

[U.S. Securities Exchange Commission]

Social Security Online

Comment

http://www.ssa.gov/

Check out the stylish Web page of the Social Security Administration. Examples of the most helpful resources:

About Social Security's benefits
Medicare information
Facts and figures
Forms
Our agency and its history
Financial status of our programs
Services for employers and businesses
Laws and regulations
Public information resources

[Social Security Administration]

Sound Money

Comment

http://money.mpr.org/

Tap into an outstanding archive of radio interview transcripts and reports on all aspects of money management as aired nationally. Each week's program features the following segments:

"News & Views" featuring Chris Farrell, economics editor at *Business Week* magazine
"Your Money Manager," Erica Whittlinger, president of Whittlinger Capital
"Smart Choices," an in-depth view of specific personal

finance issues
"Surviving the 90s," a thoughtful essay on a subject of current significance
"Buyers Market," a consumer-oriented feature

[Minnesota Public Radio]

Standard & Poor's

Comment   http://www.stockinfo.standardpoor.com/

Free access to investment data, including Standard & Poor's Stock Reports, the Standard & Poor's Equity Indices, and feature articles on investing.

[Standard & Poor's/The McGraw-Hill Companies]

Stock Quotes

Comment   http://www.lombard.com/PACenter/

Registered users have free access to valuable investment data, including:

Delayed quotes for stocks and options and basic information on over 7,000 companies
Graphs and charts of over 7,000 stocks and indices
Zacks Investment Research
QuickQuote generates price comparisons from a database of more than 1,500 term life and annuity plans

[Lombard Brokerage Inc.]

Stock Quotes (APL)

Comment   http://www.secapl.com/cgi-bin/qs

Check stock quotes (15-minute delay). Great for student investment projects. Links to online financial planning and saving calculators provide students with tools to compute the results of their investment decisions.

[CheckFree Investment Services]

Supply and Demand

Comment   http://www.mcrel.org/connect/plus/supdem.html

Students grappling with a real-world purchasing decision encounter the law of supply and demand in this thought-provoking simulation. Teachers can download the complete lesson plan to guide the discussion.

[McREL]

Comment	**Tax Prophet** http://www.taxprophet.com/pubs/pubs.html A great archive of the Tax Prophet's writings, from his weekly "Tax Man" column in the *San Francisco Examiner* to scholarly articles written for the *Journal of Taxation*. One of the best sites on the net for practical tax-related information. [Robert L. Sommers]
Comment	**Use Less Stuff** http://cygnus-group.com/ULS/Current_ULS_Reports/Reports.html Parkinson's Law of Garbage states, "Garbage expands to fill the receptacles available for its containment." This Web site may keep Parkinson from prevailing. *The ULS Report*, a bimonthly paper and online newsletter, seeks to reduce waste, conserve resources, and prevent pollution. Each issue is filled with practical articles, such as tips for operating kitchen appliances for maximum efficiency. [Partners for Environmental Progress]
Comment	**Wall Street Journal Classroom Edition** http://info.wsj.com/classroom/ Though obviously a promotional piece for its financial newspaper, this site does contain valuable resources for teaching about the U.S. economy and investing. Be sure to check out the "Teacher Resources" section for useful instructional tips. [Dow Jones Co. & Merrill Lynch]
Comment	**White House** http://www.whitehouse.gov/WH/Welcome.html Of course, this official Web site includes some public relations materials for the President and Vice President currently in power, but there is enough here to make it a worthwhile visit even for members of the loyal opposition. Students (and teachers) can send messages to the President and Vice President. (Don't expect a personal reply, though a volunteer or staff member does usually send some form of response.) The history of the White House and information on past Presidents and their families can be found in this attractive Web site. [The White House]

ELECTRONIC MAILING LISTS: CONSUMER ECONOMICS

Many electronic mailing lists focus on topics of interest to consumer economics teachers and students. It is easy to subscribe. For example, to subscribe to the mailing list CONSSCI for consumer educators:

Send an e-mail message to: LISTSERV@LSV.UKY.EDU

Usually it is best to leave the "Subject" line blank. If your e-mail software requires an entry in the subject line, simply type a period.

Enter the message: subscribe CONSSCI John Doe

Remember to enter your name instead of John Doe.

The format for the message is: subscribe <List_Name> <Your_Full_Name>

CON205
Student forum for Syracuse University consumer science class
E-mail to: LISTSERV@LISTSERV.SYR.EDU

Conssci
Consumer science list, of interest to consumer educators
E-mail to: LISTSERV@LSV.UKY.EDU

Consumer-Forum
General discussion of consumer issues
E-mail to: MAJORDOMO@IGC.ORG

Consumer-Studies
Advertising and consumption newsletter
E-mail to: MAILBASE@MAILBASE.AC.UK

E_Invest
Electronic journal for investors
E-mail to: LISTSERV@VM.TEMPLE.EDU

Publabor
Discussion of labor and labor unions in the public sector
E-mail to: LISTSERV@RELAY.DOIT.WISC.EDU

Sens
Research on consumer choice and sensory perceptions
E-mail to: LISTSERV@LISTSERV.RL.AC.UK

Tap-Info
Taxpayer Information Project from the Ralph Nader folks
E-mail to: LISTSERV@ESSENTIAL.ORG

Tch-Econ
Forum for college-level economics teachers
E-mail to: MAJORDOMO@MAJORDOMO.ELON.EDU

Newsgroups: Consumer Economics

alt.consumers.experiences	Consumer information exchange
alt.consumers.free-stuff	The price is right
alt.housing.nontrad	Different approaches to housing
americast.usa-today.money	"Money" section from USA Today Online
misc.consumers	Good source for general consumer-related discussion
misc.consumers.frugal-living	Getting by on less
misc.consumers.house	Wise advice on house buying, maintenance, etc.
misc.kids.consumers	The buying power of young folks
misc.invest.funds	Discussions of mutual funds and other investments
misc.invest.real-estate	Forum for real estate investors
rec.bicycles	Some useful advice on selection and maintenance of bicycles
rec.bicycles.off-road	Mountain bike discussion

SOCIOLOGY

BEST WEB SITES: SOCIOLOGY

Comment	**African American Male Research**
	http://www.tomco.net/~afrimale/
	This scholarly E-zine (electronic magazine) is dedicated to ferreting out the latest research on African-American males from a variety of disciplines. Archived articles include "The Representation of the Black Male in Film" and "The State of the Black Male in America: 1996."
	[Chris Booker, Editor]
Comment	**American Sociological Association**
	http://www.asanet.org/
	The home page of the major national organization of sociologists provides information about membership services, publications, and activities of A.S.A. There is a section of instructional materials, but none of it is free.
	[American Sociological Association]
Comment	**Book of Visions**
	http://newciv.org/worldtrans/GIB/BOV/BOVTOP.HTML
	This encyclopedia of social inventions warehouses a remarkable package of innovations that have been proposed for dealing with a variety of social issues. Ideas are catalogued into 25 topic areas, such as housing, crime, welfare, peace schemes, and dealing with the aged. Lots of thought-provoking ideas for student activities can be gleaned from this archive.
	[Institute for Social Inventions]
Comment	**Career Magazine**
	http://www.careermag.com/
	Various Web pages helpful in selecting and pursuing a career are linked through this E-zine. The Job Openings Database is well indexed, updated daily, and easily searchable. Focus is primarily upon jobs requiring a college education.
	[Career Magazine]

Comment	*Census Bureau* http://www.census.gov/ This visually appealing, concise, quick-loading Web site contains eleven major areas related to studying U.S. demographics: News, Access Tools, Subjects A to Z, Search, CenStats-CenStore, Just for Fun, About the Census Bureau, User Manual, New on the Site, Population Clock, Economic Clock. Every minute the Population Clock provides updated estimates of both the U.S. and world population. [U.S. Census Bureau]
Comment	*Centers for Disease Control and Prevention* http://www.cdc.gov/ This site is probably the best source for current statistics on the incidence of HIV/AIDS and sexually transmitted diseases. Detailed data are presented in easily readable formats. [Department of Health and Human Services]
Comment	*Comparative Religion* http://weber.u.washington.edu/~madin/CRELIG2.HTML# Christ Thinkers This massive clearinghouse provides dozens of links to information-packed Web sources on all aspects of the major world religions. No frills or fancy graphics, but any examination of world religions must include a visit to this site. [Mike Madin, University of Washington]
Comment	*Consumer Culture* http://www.gold.ac.uk/~soa01ds/consumer.htm Consumer culture and related topics such as consumption, leisure, and everyday life are the focus of this collection. An extensive bibliography of related books and journal articles and a list of researchers and contacts will provide useful background information. [Don Slater, Department of Sociology, Goldsmiths College University of London]

Comment	**County & City Data Books** http://www.lib.virginia.edu/socsci/ccdb/ This rich site, filled with raw data from the 1988 and 1994 County and City Data Books, provides a multitude of customized reports that can be generated online. The possibilities for generating and comparing state or county demographic changes from 1988 and 1994 support an infinite number of sociological research projects. [University of Virginia Library]
Comment	**Creating Peaceable Families** http://www.benjerry.com/esr/peaceable-index.html The focus of this noteworthy site is teaching kids to handle conflict constructively. K-12 activities for teaching both conflict resolution and peace-making skills are included, as well as suggested all-school projects for creating a more peaceable climate. The site maintains a list of professional development workshops related to teaching conflict resolution skills. The "Kids' Conscious Acts of Peace Project" features positive efforts students have taken to resolve conflicts nonviolently and creatively. The cute graphics can be a bit slow loading. [Educators for Social Responsibility and Ben & Jerry's]
Comment	**Crime Statistics Site** http://www.crime.org/ A user-friendly "Crime Statistics Tutorial" addresses topics as: Where do crime data come from? How accurate are crime data? What are crime rates? The site also provides a respectable number of links to other sites with information on historical criminal statistics, county, city, state, national, and international crime statistics. Though designed for law enforcement agencies, criminologists, and policy makers, there is ample instructional content here to enrich sociology class discussions. [Regina Schekall]

	Culture and Society of Mexico
Comment	http://www.public.iastate.edu/~rjsalvad/scmfaq/scmfaq.html
	How are prehispanic calendars interpreted? What is the origin of the term "gringo"? Answers are found in this splendid collection of Web links about the society and culture of Mexico. With the appropriate plug-ins, visitors may hear the same greeting in five languages: Castellano, English, Maya, Nahuatl, Zapoteco. A large segment of the site consists of indexed messages from the USENET newsgroup, soc.culture.mexican. Though not all links are in English, enough are to make it worthwhile, even for the Spanish-impaired.
	[Víctor Mendoza Grado and Ricardo Salvador, newsgroup unmoderators]
	Drug Enforcement Administration
Comment	http://www.usdoj.gov/dea/deahome.html
	Is the use of marijuana up or down? What are the "new" substances popular among drug users? What are the supply and demand patterns? Obtain the most current statistics on trends in drug abuse.
	[U.S. Department of Justice]
	Durkheim Pages
Comment	http://www.lang.uiuc.edu/RelSt/Durkheim/Durkheim Home.html
	Devoted to preserving the work of Emile Durkheim (1858-1917), the noted French philosopher and sociologist, this scholarly Web page includes many items of interest to the sociology teacher or student. Among the features:
	A brief biography of Durkheim A timeline describing important events related to Durkheim and the Third French Republic A biographical dictionary of Durkheim's antecedents and contemporaries A glossary of terms and concepts important to the understanding of Durkheim's works Complete texts of Durkheim's works, both in the original French and English translations A complete bibliography of Durkheim's published works, including the original French as well as existing English translations

A list of Durkheim's lecture courses given at Bordeaux and Paris

[Robert Alun Jones, University of Illinois in Urbana-Champaign]

Fads '80s vs. '90s

Comment

http://www.thejack.nau.edu/032096/Life1.html

Remember Soul Train, "Gag me with a spoon," big hair, and parachute pants? They've been replaced in the 1990s by The Grind, "Don't go there," "The Rachel," and baggy corduroys. The fads and fancies of these two decades are well documented in this electronic time capsule.

[The Lumberjack]

Family Fishbowl

Comment

http://www.wholefamily.com/fishbowl/index.html

Professional counselors have constructed this splendid, award-winning electronic magazine. There is something for every family member here. Many articles present a real world problem, followed by the professionals' analyses and suggestions. This format could be adapted for classroom use, encouraging students to analyze the problem and generate solutions before sharing the experts' advice. Recent features have included:

> Now That We Are Divorcing
> You Can't Make Anyone Love You...
> Personal Responsibility
> Ten Things Never to Do in a Marriage
> How to Fight Fairly in Marriage

[Whole Family Center]

For the People and the Press

Comment

http://www.people-press.org/cov2.htm

An independent opinion research group provides data archives on public attitudes toward press, politics, and public policy issues. Most studies focus upon the public reactions to major news stories.

[Times Mirror Center for the People & the Press, The Pew Charitable Trusts]

Comment	**Future Culture** http://www.wcpworld.com:80/future/culture.htm Useful content in this well-designed Web site on understanding the variety of world cultures should provide valuable teaching possibilities for K-12 students. Special features include a culture quiz and links to all the countries in the world. [World Cafe]
Comment	**Gallup Organization** http://www.gallup.com/ The international polling organization posts a few of its most recent survey results at its home page. [The Gallup Organization]
Comment	**Gender & Society** http://WWW.Trinity.Edu/~mkearl/gender.html This is an excellent starting point for branching to Web resources on the role of gender in various world cultures. An extensive listing of links is organized in the following categories: How Much Has Changed? Feminism and Its Backlash Violence Against Women Organizing for Change Her Story: Rethinking History from Females' Perspectives [Michael C. Kearl, Trinity University]
Comment	**Genealogy Home Page** http://www.genhomepage.com/ Many social studies teachers have incorporated genealogy projects into their classes as a tool for making sociology or history personally relevant to students. This huge resource guide is an excellent starting point for assembling genealogy instructional materials, including some good basic tutorials on genealogical research. [Stephen A. Wood]

Comment	### GeroWeb
	http://www.iog.wayne.edu/GeroWeb.html
	Browse topic areas or conduct keyword searches of this massive virtual library on gerontology and aging. Little original material, but lots of valuable links that might otherwise be overlooked.
	[Wayne State University Institute of Gerontology]
Comment	### Judaism and Jewish Resources
	http://shamash.nysernet.org/trb/judaism.html
	A well-organized, virtual gateway to numerous Internet resources on Judaism and Jewish culture and history. Several intriguing sources on Yiddish language and culture are listed.
	[Andrew Tannenbaum]
Comment	### Justice Information Center
	http://www.ncjrs.org/
	Bookmark this robust repository for the latest information on crime, law enforcement, and the justice system. It is a well-designed, easy-to-use resource. Read the reports professionals use to decide what works. Major topic areas:
	Corrections Courts Crime Prevention Criminal Justice Statistics Drugs and Crime International Juvenile Justice Law Enforcement Research and Evaluation Victims
	[National Criminal Justice Reference Service]
Comment	### Life Expectancy
	http://www.disccent.com/socsec/life_exp.html
	A female born in 1940 had a projected life expectancy of 65.7 years; her granddaughter, born in 1995, can expect to see her 79th birthday. Check this site for projected life expectancies for persons born or turning 65, anytime between 1940 and 2070.
	[Michael Rosenberg, Discussion Central]

Comment	**Looking at Different Cultures** http://www.mcrel.org/connect/plus/multi.html A few lesson plans to help students examine other cultures objectively. Links to related resources are also provided. [McREL, Office of Educational Research and Improvement, Department of Education]
Comment	**Marriage & Family Processes** http://WWW.Trinity.Edu/~mkearl/family.html "The 'traditional' nuclear family, with a husband wage-earner, wife homemaker, and dependent children, now accounts for less than 10 percent of all American households," according to data from this information-filled clearinghouse. Much valuable original information and hypertext links to scholarly sites enrich the study of marriage and family processes. [Michael C. Kearl, Trinity University]
Comment	**National Archive of Criminal Justice Data** *A+* http://www.icpsr.umich.edu/NACJD/archive.html A true treasure chest of data related to crime and justice in America. The site offers over 500 data collections related to criminal justice. Most of the data can be downloaded. Users must pay attention to the date each data set was collected because some are relatively old. [Bureau of Justice Statistics, National Institute of Justice, and the Office of Juvenile Justice and Delinquency Prevention]
Comment	**National Center on Addiction and Substance Abuse** http://www.casacolumbia.org/home.htm C.A.S.A. is a multidisciplinary, think/action tank with a mission of combating all forms of substance abuse: alcohol, illegal drugs, pills, and tobacco. Its Web page includes current research on the costs, impact, and prevention and treatment of substance abuse. [National Center on Addiction and Substance Abuse at Columbia University]

Comment	National Clearinghouse for Alcohol and Drug Information
	http://www.health.org/pressrel/index.htm
	Turn to the source journalists use for up-to-date information about alcohol and substance abuse. Database searches provide access to thousands of documents related to substance abuse.
	[U.S. Department of Health & Human Services]
Comment	Native American News
	http://www.nanews.org/
	A weekly, online newsletter, "Wotanging Ikche," was created as "a way of keeping the brothers and sisters who share our Spirit informed about current events within the lives of those who walk the Red Road." The most current issue and an archive of past ones provide a view of contemporary Native Americans, their world, culture, and beliefs, that will seldom be seen in mainstream publications.
	[Wolf's Den Educational Services and Gary Night Owl]
Comment	Native Nations
	http://www.pitt.edu/~lmitten/indians.html#nations
	A useful compendium of Internet-accessible information on individual Native American nations, from the Alaskan Haida, Tlingit, and Tsimshian peoples to the Seminole tribe of Florida. An alphabetical listing by nation or tribe provides dozens of links. An extensive listing of native organizations and urban Indian centers could prove valuable in arranging possible classroom speakers or field trips.
	[Lisa Mittenat, University of Pittsburgh]
Comment	Native Web
	http://web.maxwell.syr.edu/nativeweb/
	Dedicated to the preservation of the culture and history of the earth's indigenous peoples, this virtual gateway has organized hundreds of Web links into logical categories, such as art, dance, health, history, language, music, religion/spirituality, and women. Alternative indexes group the links by

geographic region or nationality. Separate branches list related newsletters and journals, bibliographies, literature, and organizations. This is an ambitious undertaking; fortunately the creators have organized the mass information well to make it readily accessible.

[David Cole]

Russian Proverbs and Sayings

Comment

http://www.friends-partners.org/friends/literature/russian-proverbs.htmlopt-tables-mac-english-

"An empty barrel makes the greatest sound," "All are not cooks that walk with long knives," and "Eggs cannot teach a hen" are samples of the pithy Russian proverbs and folk sayings housed in this unique site. The content is excerpted from M. Dubrovin's book *A Book of English and Russian Proverbs and Sayings* (Moscow, "Prosvesheniye," 1993).

[Natasha Bulashova & Greg Cole, Friends and Partners]

Social Statistics Briefing Room

Comment

http://www.whitehouse.gov/fsbr/ssbr.html

What percentage of the U.S. population falls below the poverty level? How many people own their own homes? Answers to these and many more questions can be found in the Social Statistics Briefing Room. This unique clearinghouse draws upon a variety of U.S. governmental agencies for statistics on general demographics, crime, education, and health.

[The White House]

Sociological Research Online

Comment

http://www.socresonline.org.uk/socresonline/

This quarterly online periodical provides discussion on assorted political, cultural, and intellectual topics.

[University of Surrey, UK]

Sociologists

Comment

http://www.pscw.uva.nl/sociosite/TOPICS/Sociologists.html

Download descriptions of the work and lives of over forty prominent sociologists, featuring excerpts from their most noted writings.

[Sociological Institute, University of Amsterdam]

	Sociology Cases Database Project
Comment	http://www.nd.edu/~dhachen/cases/
	This most useful database of sociological cases provides ample fodder for teaching sociology. The archive of cases encompasses family issues, politics, health care, school life, work, religion, community changes, and assorted other topics. An interactive forum for this innovative project provides teachers an opportunity to exchange suggestions for using cases in introductory sociology classes.
	[Wadsworth Publishing Company and David Hachen]
	Sociology of Death & Dying
Comment	http://WWW.Trinity.Edu/~mkearl/death.html
	Check out this award-winning, scholarly, but comprehensible, electronic megasite on the sociological investigation of death, its impact on social order, meaning, relationship to social organizations, and personal impact. The sections on the personal impact of death, grieving, and funerals are filled with potential instructional content. Links to many other Internet resources related to death and dying are included.
	[Michael C. Kearl, Trinity University]
	Sociology Timeline Since 1600
Comment	http://www.wwu.edu/~stephan/Schedule/302/timeline.html
	Access a timeline of major events in the evolution of sociology as a discipline. Hypertext links connect to in-depth explanations of significant events and personalities. The Web page author was not overly humble in including publication of his own work, *The Division of Territory in Society*, in the timeline of notable events. He could probably be forgiven such a lapse in humility as the full-test version is available online, though it is probably too technical to be of much use to most high school students.
	[Ed Stephan]
	Southern Native American Pow Wows
Comment	http://tqd.advanced.org/3081/
	This colorful and charming resource was a prize-winner in the ThinkQuest '96 student competition for creative Web

page designs. Three high school students have sensitively explored the topic of Southern Native American pow wows, particularly those in the Oklahoma-Texas area. Their tips on pow wow etiquette for first-timers add a unique angle on the topic. Additional information on the history of the Southern Circle, pow wow terminology, customs and courtesies, and dance styles provides a rich understanding of this lesser-known event. The list of annual pow wows should prove of interest to anyone wanting to explore the topic further.

[Chris Glazner and Roxanne Solis, North Shore High School, Houston; Geoff Weinman, Dumas High School, Houston]

Statistical Abstract of the United States

Comment

http://www.census.gov/prod/2/gen/96statab/96statab.html

This major reference guide, used by sociologists and other researchers, can be downloaded in Adobe Acrobat format. It contains extensive data on U.S. population, education, vital statistics, employment, and other areas. The hundreds of tables provide valuable data for class projects and lesson ideas.

[United States Bureau of Census]

Teaching Sociology

Comment

http://www.lemoyne.edu/ts/tsmain.html

This site contains information about the A.S.A. quarterly publication, "Teaching Sociology." Although the Table of Contents from the latest issue is posted, no articles are available online. Information on subscribing to the "Teaching Sociology" discussion group and an archive of past messages are available. These do contain some ideas which should be of interest to high school sociology teachers.

[The American Sociological Association]

Times of Our Lives

Comment

http://www.trinity.edu/~mkearl/time.html

This splendid exhibit explores the meanings we attach to time, how we monitor it, and how it shapes our thoughts and behaviors. Time pressures, "quality time," career timelines, flextime, and fears of growing old are all manifestations of the important role this concept plays in our lives and culture. Excellent content; a real winner.

[Michael C. Kearl, Department of Sociology & Anthropology, Trinity University]

Comment

Universal Black Pages

http://www.ubp.com/History/

Few realize that 95 percent of the trans-Atlantic slave trade arrived in the West Indies and Latin America. Dozens of Web links provide a cornucopia of resources pertaining to African descendants in all parts of the Americas.

[BGSI, Inc.]

Comment

Urban Legends Archive

http://www.urbanlegends.com/

Most people have heard stories of alligators appearing in the sewers of New York City. This and other "urban legends" have been circulated, orally and in print, to the point where they have become accepted as truths even though they are actually unsubstantiated. This clearinghouse contains many examples of such tales.

[Jason R. Heimbaugh]

Comment

Women in Islam Society

http://www.usc.edu/dept/MSA/humanrelations/ womeninislam/womeninso ciety.html

Clarifying the role of women in the Islam society is the purpose of this Web site. Though exclusively a text document, it does contain valuable information.

[Abdur Rahman I., Ahmadu Bello University, Nigeria]

Comment

What Is Culture?

http://www.wsu.edu:8001/vcwsu/commons/topics/culture/ culture-index.html

This basic online tutorial helps sociology students explore the definition of culture with concrete, everyday examples.

[Eric Miraglia, Richard Law, Peg Collins]

Comment	**Whole Family Center**
	http://www.wholefamily.com/
	A magnificent, colorful, fun, informative resource, covering the many sides of family life. The "Marital Center" focuses upon the large and small challenges confronting couples. Written or audio transcripts challenge users to think through several crucial marital conflicts. "Kids & Teens" and the "Parent Center" add similar content targeted toward those roles.
	[Whole Family Center]
Comment	**World Population**
	http://sunsite.unc.edu/lunarbin/worldpop
	The WorldPop clock provides 30-second updates on the estimated world and U.S. population. The data are actually based upon U.N. World Populations Estimates & Projections. Links are also provided to the U.S. Census Bureau to provide comparisons with its estimates of world and U.S. populations.
Comment	**Zero Population Growth**
	http://www.igc.apc.org/zpg/
	"Why should Americans be concerned about population growth in other parts of the world?" "Isn't it true that the United States' welfare system encourages people to have more babies?" These are two of the important questions addressed at this Web site concerned with rapid population growth and wasteful consumption. The "Pop Quiz" provides a test of knowledge of population facts, statistics, and impact. Current news items concerning population growth, U.S. federal and state legislation affecting population policy, and population information (statistics, libraries, databases) are thoroughly covered. A useful set of population-related curriculum materials provides teaching resources, research paper ideas, and suggested teaching activities.
	[Zero Population Growth, Inc.]

ELECTRONIC MAILING LISTS: SOCIOLOGY

Many electronic mailing lists focus on topics of interest to sociology teachers and students. It is easy to subscribe. For example, to subscribe to the mailing list on Southern United States Culture:

Send an e-mail message to: LISTPROC@KNUTH.MTSU.EDU

Usually it is best to leave the "Subject" line blank. If your e-mail software requires something in the subject line, simply type a period.

Enter the message: subscribe BUBBA-L John Doe

Remember to enter your name instead of John Doe.

The format for the message is: subscribe <List_Name> <Your_Full_Name>

Abslst-L
Association of Black Sociologists (moderated)
E-mail to: LISTSERV@CMUVM.CSV.CMICH.EDU

Aera-G
Social Context of Education. American Educational Research Association's (AERA) discussion list for educational sociologists
E-mail to: LISTSERV@ASUVM.INRE.ASU.EDU

Anthro-L
Discussions of anthropology
E-mail to: LISTSERV@UBVM.CC.BUFFOLO.EDU

Appsoc
Study of applied sociology
E-mail to: MAJORDOMO@INDIANA.EDU

Bubba-L
Popular culture of the Southern United States
E-mail to: LISTPROC@KNUTH.MTSU.EDU

Comm-List
Community sociology
E-mail to: LISTSERV@LISTSERV.ACSU.BUFFALO.EDU

Cjust-L
Criminal Justice
E-mail to: LISTSERV@IUBVM.UCS.INDIANA.EDU

Drugabus
Drug abuse forum
E-mail to: LISTSERV@UMAB.UMD.EDU

Econsoc
Economic Sociology
E-mail to: LISTPROC@LISTPROC.HCF.JHU.EDU

Electronic-Sociology-L
Electronic Journal of Sociology (EJS) forum
E-mail to: MAJORDOMO@COOMBS.ANU.EDU.AU

Ethno
Social interaction and communication
E-mail to: LISTSERV@RPITSVM.BITNET

Familysci
Family issues
E-mail to: LISTSERV@UKCC.UKY.EDU

Femisa
Women in the global economy
E-mail to: LISTSERV@MACH1.WLU.EDU

Folklore
Folklore discussion
E-mail to: LISTSERV@TAMVM1.TAMU.EDU

Futurec
Futurist forum
E-mail to: LISTSERV@UAFSYSB.UARK.EDU

Futurework
The future of work
E-mail to: LISTSERV@CSF.COLORADO.EDU

Gangtm
Gangs and gang-related problems
E-mail to: GANDTM-REQUEST@DHVX20.CSUDH.EDU

Gender
Study of gender and communication
E-mail: LISTSERV@VM.ITS.RPI.EDU

Homeless
Homelessness
E-mail to: LISTPROC@CSF.COLORADO.EDU

HR-OD-L
Human resource management, organizational development, and change
E-mail to: LISTSERV@KSUVM.KSU.EDU

Interact
Symbolic interaction
E-mail to: LISTPROC@SUN.SOCI.NIU.EDU

Intercul
Discussion of intercultural communication
E-mail to: LISTSERV@VM.ITS.RPI.EDU

Interper
Interpersonal and small group communication
E-mail to: LISTSERV@VM.ITS.RPI.EDU

Intvio-L
Family violence
E-mail to: LISTSERV@URIACC.URI.EDU

Lore
Folklore discussion
E-mail to: LISTSERV@NDSUVM1

Methods
Social science research methodologies
E-mail to: COMSERVE@VM.ITS.RPI.EDU

Nerdnosh
Storytelling and family fables
E-mail to: MAJORDOMO@SCRUZ.UCSC.EDU

Niatrn-L
Researchers in population aging
E-mail to: NIATRN-L@LIST.NIH.GOV

Night-L
Folklore of the supernatural
E-mail to: LISTPROC@UNICORN.ACS.TTU.EDU

Nwac-L
The ever-changing nature of work
E-mail to: LISTSERV@PSUVM.PSU.EDU

Ortrad-L
Discussion of oral traditions
E-mail to: LISTSERV@MIZZOU1.MISSOURI.EDU

Polcomm
Political communication
E-mail to: LISTSERV@VM.ITS.RPI.EDU

Popcult
Popular culture
E-mail to: MAILSERV@CAMOSUN.BC.CA

POR
Public opinion research forum
E-mail to: LISTSERV@UNC.EDU

PSN
Progressive sociologists' network
E-mail to: LISTSERV@CSF.COLORADO.EDU

REVS
Racial/ethnic violence and discrimination
E-mail to: LISTSERV@CSF.COLORADO.EDU

Ruraldev
Rural development
E-mail to: LISTSERV@KSUVM.KSU.EDU

Rursoc-L
Rural sociology
E-mail to: LISTSERV@LSV.UKY.EDU

Sixties-L
Cultural, social, and political movements of the 1960s
E-mail to: LISTPROC@JEFFERSON.VILLAGE.VIRGINIA.EDU

SO010
Introduction to sociology course discussion
E-mail to: LISTSERV%UMSLVMA.BITNET@LISTERV.NET

SO200
Sociology of deviant behavior
E-mail to: LISTSERV%UMSLVMA.BITNET@LISTERV.NET

Soced
Sociology of education
E-mail to: MAJORDOMO@LISTS.STANFORD.EDU

Soceth-L
Social ethics forum
E-mail to: LISTSERV@VM.USC.EDU

Social-Class
Social class in today's societies
E-mail to: LISTSERV@LISTSERV.UIC.EDU

Sociology
Sociological issues
E-mail to: LISTSERV@THINK.NET

Ciology-Family-L
The sociology of the family
E-mail to: LISTWSERV@LISTSERV.UTORONTO.CA

Socnet
Study of social networks
E-mail to: LISTSERV@NERVM.NERDC.UFL.EDU

Socpol-L
Social Politics electronic journal
E-mail to: LISTSERV@VMD.CSO.UIUC.EDU

Soctalk
General discussion of sociology
E-mail to: LISTSERV%UMSLVMA.BITNET@LISTERV.NET

Sportsoc
Sociological aspects of sports (moderated).
Site: Temple University, Philadelphia, USA.
E-mail to: LISTSERV@VM.TEMPLE.EDU

Teachsoc
Social science data
E-mail to: LISTSERV@MAPLE.LEMOYNE.EDU

Tecgrp-L
Technology and social behavior
E-mail to: LISTSERV@PSUVM.PSU.EDU

Urban-L
Urban planning forum
E-mail to: LISTSERV@VM.EGE.EDU.TR

Wimnet-L
Gender issues in organizations
E-mail to: LISTSERV@VM.UCS.UALBERTA.CA

ELECTRONIC JOURNALS: SOCIOLOGY

Annual Review of Sociology
http://www.annurev.org/series/sociolgy/sociolgy.htm

Canadian Journal of Sociology
http://gpu.srv.ualberta.ca/~cjscopy/cjs.html

Postmodern Culture
http://jefferson.village.Virginia.EDU:80/pmc/

Sociological Research Online
http://kennedy.soc.surrey.ac.uk/socresonline/

Newsgroups: Sociology

alt.crime	All aspects of criminal activity
alt.culture.us.1970s	Culture of the United States in the 1970s
alt.culture.us.asian-indian	Culture of the Asian-Indian in the U.S.
alt.culture.us.southwest	Culture of the Southwest United States
alt.culture.www	Discussion of the Web's own culture
alt.discrimination	Affirmative action, prejudice, bigotry
alt.folklore.science	Folklore of science
alt.folklore.urban	Urban legends
alt.hindu	The Hindu religion
alt.law-enforcement	Discussion of laws and law enforcement
alt.native	General discussion of Native American issues
alt.politics.drinking-age	Opinions on legal drinking age
alt.prisons	The penal system
alt.religion.islam	Discussion of Islamic religion
alt.support.ex-cult	For ex-cult members, their families and friends
soc.culture.african.american	African-American culture

Newsgroups: Sociology (Continued)

soc.culture.asian.american	Culture of Asian Americans
soc.culture.indian	Discussion of India and Indian culture
soc.culture.jewish	Jewish culture and religion
soc.culture.mexican.american	Culture of Mexican Americans
soc.culture.misc	Discussion of other cultures
soc.culture.palestine	Palestinian people, politics, and culture
soc.culture.usa	Contemporary United States culture
soc.feminism	Moderated discussion of feminist issues
soc.religion.christian	Christianity
soc.religion.eastern	Discussion of Eastern religions
soc.religion.hindu	Discussion of Hindu philosophy & culture (moderated)
soc.religion.islam	Islamic religon (moderated)
soc.religion.quaker	Society of Friends theology and culture
soc.religion.unitarian-univ	Discussion of Unitarian-Universalism
soc.women	Women's concerns
talk.politics.drugs	Discussion of the political issues of drug control
talk.religion.buddhism	Buddhist religion and philosophy

PSYCHOLOGY

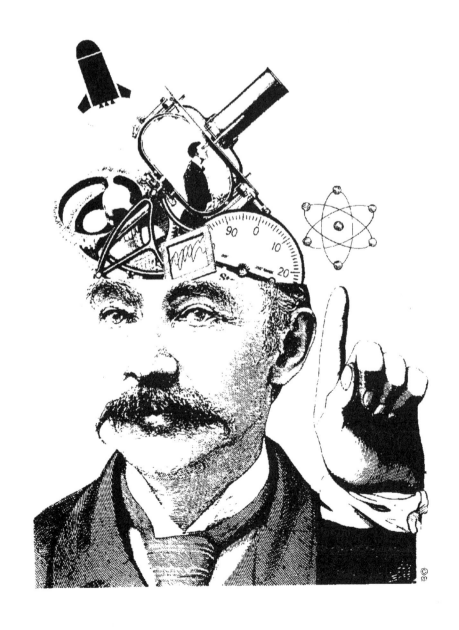

BEST WEB SITES: PSYCHOLOGY

Comment	**ADOL: Adolescence Directory On-Line** http://education.indiana.edu/cas/adol/adol.html If it is about adolescence, it will be found in this complete electronic resource directory. Extensive listings are organized under the following file headings: What's New? Conflict and Violence Resources about Violence Prevention and Peer Mediation Mental Health Issues Health Risks Counselor Resources Teens Only [Center for Adolescent Studies]
Comment	**Advanced Placement Psychology** HTTP://www.collegeboard.org/ap/psychology/html/indx001.html Acquire information about the Advanced Placement Psychology Examination along with sample items. [College Board Online]
Comment	**American Psychological Society** http://psych.hanover.edu/APS/ Over 3,100 events in the history of psychology are listed in this historical database. Submit a day of the year and retrieve a list of historical psychology-related events occurring on that date. These can be used as attention grabbers by posting one each day. [American Psychological Society]
Comment	**Auditory Perception** http://lecaine.music.mcgill.ca/~welch/auditory/Auditory.html This multimedia presentation of assorted topics in auditory perception includes fun and interesting demonstrations on psychoacoustics and several online experiments on pitch perception, auditory scene analysis, musical illusions, and absolute pitch. An excellent teaching resource! [Music Faculty, McGill University]

A+

Comment	**Autism** http://www.autism.org/ Home page of the Center for the Study of Autism which "provides information about autism to parents and professionals and conducts research on the efficacy of various therapeutic interventions." A very thorough archive of information on all aspects of autism. Although some items are fairly technical, many are targeted to a general audience. [Center for the Study of Autism]
Comment	**Basic Neural Functioning** http://psych.hanover.edu/Krantz/neurotut.html A collection of tutorials on basic neural functions. Current topics include: Quiz on Structure of the Neuron and Brain Study and Check your Knowledge of the Human Brain Review of Physical Factors Involved in the Action Potential Glossary of terms [John H. Krantz, Hanover College]
Comment	**Brainstorm** http://www.mcp.com/ssi/ssint/iqgame/ A splendid collection of challenging brainteasers and puzzles for stretching the mind. [Simon & Schuster Interactive]
Comment	**Burying Freud** http://www.shef.ac.uk/uni/projects/gpp/burying_freud.html Students and teachers can access this ongoing, lively debate on the effectiveness of psychotherapy and the empirical validity of Freud's theory. An extensive exchange of online correspondence has accumulated. Good food for thought. [Ian Pitchford]
Comment	**Canadian Journal of Behavioural Science** http://www.cycor.ca/Psych/cjbs.htm The full-text, online copy of the scholarly research journal features articles on a variety of psychological topics. It is

important to remember that electronic publications are subject to the same copyright restrictions as any paper journal would be. French and non-frames-based versions of the journal are also available. The C.J.B.S. is clearly in the vanguard, demonstrating what academic journals can become in the next decade.

[Canadian Psychological Association]

Comment

Circle of Thought

http://hawaii.cogsci.uiuc.edu/invent/Circle_of_thought.html

This text-heavy, brief introduction to cognitive psychology examines the basic components of thinking: describe, elaborate, decide, plan, and act.

[Gary Bradshaw]

Comment

Classroom Assistant

http://web.wwnorton.com/norton/grip.html

Though created as an online teachers' manual for Henry Gleitman's Psychology textbook, there is much here of interest to teachers who are not using his book. Suggested Internet resources and downloadable electronic transparencies are included for each topic area.

[W. W. Norton, Company]

Comment

Creative Quotations

http://www.shentel.net/baertracks/

Over 1,000 quotations pertaining to creativity are housed in this charming Web site. Well-organized, logical indexes permit browsing by several categories (e.g., by profession) or via keyword searches.

[Baertracks Creative Impulses]

Comment

Creativity, Innovation and Problem Solving

http://www.shentel.net/baertracks/

A basic tutorial on the creative process provides practical suggestions for effective, innovative critical thinking following four elements:

"TRUE Creativity and Innovation consists of
SEEING what everyone else has seen,

THINKING what no one else has thought, and
DOING what no one else has dared!"

Excellent examples of each aspect of the creative thinking process are included.

[Quantum Books]

Creativity Web

Comment

http://www.ozemail.com.au/~caveman/Creative/index.html

This massive resource is a gold mine of information on creativity and innovation. Check out these topic headings for many mind-stimulating instructional resources:

> Creativity Basics
> The Brain and the Creative Process
> Idea Recording Methods
> Your Creative Space
> Mental Workout Center
> Idea and Problem Bank
> Creative Genius Gallery
> Children's Corner
> Quotations

[Charles Cave]

Critical Thinking in Psychology

Comment

http://gateway1.gmcc.ab.ca/~digdonn/psych104/think.htm

A psychology instructor has devised a fine tutorial on critical thinking skills needed by psychology students. Topics include designing studies, asking effective research questions, and becoming an objective consumer of psychology in the media.

[Nancy Digdon, Grant MacEwan Community College]

Depression Central

Comment

http://www.psycom.net/depression.central.html

This electronic guide provides introductory as well as advanced information on depressive disorders. A well-organized network of links is provided to dozens of Internet resources related to depression and its treatment.

[Ivan Goldberg, MD]

Comment	## Depression: Quick Reference Guide
	http://www.mentalhealth.com/bookah/p44-dq.html
	Though written for mental health professionals, this information-packed resource provides a primer on clinical depression. Such items as the "Risk Factors for Depression" provide valuable supplementary teaching content for psychology teachers.
	[Phillip W. Long, M.D., Internet Mental Health]
Comment	## Down Syndrome
	http://www.nas.com/downsyn/information.html
	A thorough, sensitive compilation of up-to-date information on Down Syndrome.
	[Down Syndrome listserv]
Comment	## Eating Disorders
	http://www.something-fishy.com/ed.htm
	This attractive, colorful, quick-loading Web site provides a good general introduction to the risks, symptoms, consequences, and treatment of eating disorders.
	[Something Fishy Web site]
Comment	## Enchanted Mind
	http://enchantedmind.com/
	This imaginative collection is stuffed with mind-stretching puzzles, humor, and inspirational content which can be adapted for psychology and other social studies classes. Extensive resources, some original, others linked to external sites, are housed in the following categories:
	Zen of pondering puzzles Latest additions & creative techniques Quantum brain and creativity Weekly ponderable puzzle Attributes of a creative mind Random acts of silliness Sample of weekly puzzle sets Format of puzzles offered Creative living Some great creative links
	[J. L. Read]

Comment	### Exploratorium Exhibits http://www.exploratorium.edu/imagery/exhibits.html Can you pick the correct image of a penny from a dozen different pictures? This is but one online experiment available in this museum exhibit demonstrating psychological concepts related to perception and memory. A useful site if students have Internet access or if you can capture the graphic images. [The Exploratorium]

Comment	### Facts for Families
	
	http://www.aacap.org/factsFam/
	
	This valuable source on psychiatric disorders affecting children and adolescents includes concise information sheets on topics, such as:
	
	    Children and Divorce
	    Teenagers with Eating Disorders
	    Teens: Alcohol and Other Drugs
	    The Depressed Child
	    Children and Grief
	    Children and TV Violence
	    Children of Alcoholics
	    Stepfamily Problems
	    Responding to Child Sexual Abuse
	    Children and AIDS
	    When Children Have Children
	    Children's Sleep Problems
	    Helping Children After a Disaster
	    Manic-Depressive Illness in Teens
	    Children of Parents with Mental Illness
	    The Influence of Music and Rock Videos
	
	[American Academy of Child & Adolescent Psychiatry]

Comment	### General Psychology http://www.indiana.edu:80/~iuepsyc/P103Psyc.html Innovating what is probably a harbinger of the Cyber-college of the next century, Susan Shapiro has created an online college-level course in General Psychology. The course can be taken for college credit through Indiana University East, or just completed independently for personal knowledge and no formal credit. Psychology teachers can pull up her Web page

to view the course syllabus, assignments, quizzes, experiments, and Web links for additional information. It is interesting just to see how her course is packaged.

[Susan Shapiro, Indiana University East]

Comment

HabitSmart

http://www.cts.com:80/~habtsmrt/

This helpful and convenient repository provides abundant information about "addictive behavior, theories of habit endurance and habit change, as well as tips for effectively managing problematic habitual behavior." Dr. Westermeyer's "Self Scoring Alcohol Check-up" encourages drinkers to assess whether their behavior has become problematic and warrants modification. His "Tipping the Scale" module invites users to examine their own attitudes toward their addictive behaviors. An extensive jumplist to other Web resources on addiction is maintained.

[Robert Westermeyer, Ph.D.]

Comment

How to Stay Stressed

http://matia.stanford.edu/~pinto/stress.html

"Anyone as stressed as you must be working very hard and, therefore, is probably doing something very crucial." Such tongue-in-cheek advice is the fodder of this amusing Web page. Share these gems with your overly serious colleagues and students.

[De Anza Health Office]

Comment

How to Survive Unbearable Stress

http://www.teachhealth.com/

This delightful, online book was written specifically for young people (probably most suitable for high school). Charming illustrations and down-to-earth language enrich the academically credible content of the stress tutorial. Checklists invite active participation and application. Permission is granted by the authors to copy their original material for classroom use.

[Steve Burns, M.D. & Kimberley Burns]

Comment	**HyperState Online** http://www.ruf.rice.edu/~lane/hyperstat/contents.html Tune in to an excellent online tutorial on basic statistics. The chapters on probability and normal distribution should be helpful for high school psychology students. [David Lane, Rice University]
Comment	**Internet Depression Resources List** http://www.execpc.com/~corbeau/ This fresh, user-friendly compilation of Internet resources on clinical depression and suicide is highly recommended. It appears to be regularly updated. [Dennis Taylor]
Comment	**Internet Mental Health** http://www.mentalhealth.com/ A free encyclopedia of mental health is filled with informative Web pages. The online interactive diagnostic simulation for mood disorders, substance abuse, and personality disorders provides an educational glimpse of the thought process required of mental health professionals in making a professional diagnosis. [Phillip Long, Canadian psychologist]
Comment	**Internet Psychology Laboratory** http://kahuna.psych.uiuc.edu/ipl/index.html Explore this multimedia, interactive laboratory which features a collection of psychology-related experiments, mostly on visual or auditory perception. Only about a dozen activities are currently online. Hopefully, it will be expanded. [L. J. Trejo, G. Bradshaw, M. Hamman, C. A. N. Fitzgerald, C. Currie, and J. I. K. McClure; University of Illinois]
Comment	**Knowledge Exchange Network** http://www.mentalhealth.org/ KEN fulfills its promise to serve as a "national, one-stop source of information and resources on prevention, treat-

A+

ment, and rehabilitation services for mental illness." It offers an electronic bulletin board where users can join discussions on mental health or search a massive library of information files. This valuable resource includes exhaustive lists of mental health advocacy organizations, federal, state, and local mental health agencies, mental health organizations, and national clearinghouses.

[U.S. Department of Health and Human Services]

Living in a Social World

Comment

http://miavx1.muohio.edu/~shermarc/p324news.htmlx

A practical tutorial on interpreting the news from a social psychology perspective was developed by college psychology students. Several current news stories are incorporated into the learning activity.

[Miami University (Ohio)]

Major Mental Disorders

Comment

http://delta.is.tcu.edu/~SBAmling/mmd1.html

This site provides basic information on mental illness with a brief description of the major mental disorders, including links to pertinent Internet resources.

[Susan B. Amling, *The Dallas Morning News*]

Mental Health Net

Comment

http://www.cmhc.com/

This exceptional starting point for locating information related to mental health features over 6,000 individual resources. It is a well-organized, user-friendly site covering mental disorders and links to electronic journals and self-help resources.

[CMHC Systems, sponsor]

Meta-Self: A Visual Aid to Being Human

Comment

http://www.dnai.com/model/

This interactive, imaginative Web site focuses upon metaphor as a writing and critical thinking skill. An intriguing model for viewing the human mind and interpersonal perception is presented. Fairly detailed lesson plans for teaching the model are included, but instructors will have to work through the interactive tutorial to gain a full understanding of the process before attempting to teach it.

[Peter Carleton]

Comment

Mind Tools

http://www.gasou.edu/psychweb/mtsite/index.html

Do not miss this site! It is one of the best resources on personal mastery you'll find, either on the Net or elsewhere. Well-written, entertaining, and practical tutorials guide users through basic life skills, such as stress management, communication skills, and enhancing creativity. Mind Tools Resources include:

> Techniques to Help You Think Excellently:
>   Problem Solving Techniques & Analytical Methods
> Information Skills
>   Improving Your Memory
>   Increasing Creativity
> Skills for High Performance Living
>   Mastering Stress
>   Time Management Skills
>   Achieving Ambitions with Goal Setting
>   Planning Skills
>   Motivation & Winning Attitudes
>   Communication Skills
>   Leadership Skills
>   Fitness & Health
> Practical Psychology
>   Interpersonal Psychology
>   Management Psychology
>   Sports Psychology
>   Psychometric Tests

[Mind Tools Ltd.]

Comment

Moderation Movement

http://comnet.org/mm/

This self-help resource seeks to assist persons wishing to reduce their level of drinking and make positive changes in their lifestyles.

[Moderation Management Network, Inc.]

	National Clearinghouse for Alcohol and Drug Information
Comment	http://www.health.org/
	This colorful, perky resource center offers excellent content on the prevention of alcohol and substance abuse. Using imaginative graphics and plain text, many of the pages are meant to appeal to adolescents. Parents and educators can access an extensive library of online and inexpensive paper publications; a sampling of those available:
	NIDA Research Report: Anabolic Steroids A Threat to Mind and Body The Relationship between Family Structure and Adolescent Substance Use National Household Survey on Drug Abuse Fact Sheet—The National Structured Evaluation of Alcohol and Other Drug Abuse Prevention Action Steps for Parents and Caregivers Tips for Teens: Marijuana Growing Up Drug Free: Parent's Guide to Prevention
	[Center for Substance Abuse Prevention, Substance Abuse and Mental Health Services Administration, Center for Substance Abuse Treatment]
	National Institute of Mental Health
Comment	http://gopher.nimh.nih.gov/
	This valuable resource provides extensive coverage of research and legislation related to mental health, as well as information on specific mental disorders, their diagnosis, and treatment.
	[National Institute of Mental Health, U.S. Department of Health and Human Services]
	National Mental Health Association
Comment	http://www.nmha.org/
	Did you know that one in five adults suffers from some form of mental disorder, or that one in four families will have a member with a mental illness? These are just two facts from the storehouse of vital information available thorough the N.M.H.A. The National Mental Health Association is a national citizen volunteer advocacy organization focusing on mental

health and mental illnesses. It provides much valuable information on mental health advocacy, prevention, information, and public education. Several excellent factsheets are available online; many more may be ordered at no charge.

[National Mental Health Association]

NetPsych.Com

Comment

http://netpsych.com/

Designed to "explore online delivery of mental health services," this Web site includes a listing of psychologists and counselors who provide Internet-based counseling services. While most also provide more traditional mental health services, the concept does provide interesting professional and ethical challenges which might be discussed by students. This artfully done Web site also includes other mental health resources, including lists of bulletin boards, self-help chat rooms, online advice columns, and articles on electronic counseling services. This certainly represents a controversial, nontraditional approach. Is it the wave of the future or simply another commercial exploration of Cyperspace technology?

[Leonard Holmes, Ph.D.]

Neuroscience for Kids

Comment

http://weber.u.washington.edu/~chudler/neurok.html

A+

Students can make a model of the brain, compete in a neuroscience treasure hunt, stretch their minds with challenging brain games, or develop their short-term memory. This exciting Web site provides elementary or secondary students and teachers with active learning lessons of the highest educational merit. The "Explore the Brain and Spinal Cord" tutorial posseses a depth, breadth, and richness found in few educational resources, online or in any other media. A real gem; don't miss this one!

[Eric H. Chudler, Department of Anesthesiology, University of Washington]

Parenting

Comment

http://ericps.ed.uiuc.edu/npin/npinhome.html

The National Parent Information Network (NPIN) provides an enormous body of information to parents and others interested in parenting. A massive amount of data is accessible here. Full-text editions of some items are available. "AskERIC" permits users to submit questions which are answered by staff members within a couple of days. Full-text booklets on parenting and children are available.

[ERIC Clearinghouse on Urban Education; ERIC Clearinghouse on Elementary and Early Childhood Education]

Comment

Personality and Consciousness

http://www.wynja.com/giganto/psych/theorists.html

This inviting, comprehensive guide to the major personality theorists examines the lives and work of Sigmund Freud, Alfred Adler, Carl Rogers, B. F. Skinner, Carl Jung, and others. Excerpts from their major writings, as well as biographical information, are included. Intriguing photographs of the theorists continuously morph from one to another on the home page.

[Eric Pettifor]

Comment

Personality Project

http://fas.psych.nwu.edu/personality.html

Provides references to many helpful links related to personality theory and research. A few course syllabi from personality theory and research courses are included. While much of the content is too advanced for high school students, teachers may still find some useful background.

[William Revelle, Department of Psychology, Northwestern University]

Comment

Positive Reinforcement: A Self-Instructional Exercise

A+

http://server.bmod.athabascau.ca/html/prtut/reinpair.htm

This excellent, self-pacing tutorial on the concept of positive reinforcement incorporates examples and nonexamples as an effective instructional device. Hopefully, more online tutorials of this caliber will be posted in the future.

[Lyle Grant, Athabasca University]

Comment	**Post-Traumatic Stress Disorder** http://www.dartmouth.edu/dms/ptsd/ This national clearinghouse strives to cover all research and educational materials on P.T.S.D. While much is not downloadable, a few general publications should be of value to psychology teachers and their students. [National Center for Post-Traumatic Stress Disorder, U.S. Department of Veterans Affairs]
Comment	**Post-Traumatic Stress Resources Page** http://www.long-beach.va.gov/ptsd/stress.html A respectable listing of resources related to post-traumatic stress disorder. [Carl T. Hayden Veterans Affairs Medical Center]
Comment	**Psychiatric Times** http://www.mentalhealth.com/fr50.html This online magazine features a broad array of articles on mental health. In-depth, scholarly articles are added each month. [CME Corporation]
Comment	**Psychology in Daily Life** http://www.apa.org/pubinfo/pubinfo.html Several practical brochures are on topics of interest to students, some of which are: Sexual Harassment: Myths and Realities Controlling Anger before It Controls You What You Should Know about Women and Depression Answers to Questions about Panic Disorder [American Psychological Association]
Comment	**Psychology of Religion** http://www.gasou.edu/psychweb/psyrelig/psyrelig.htm Users gain a good, general introduction to the psychology of religion, mostly via links to other Web sites. [Michael E. Nielsen, Ph.D.]

Psycholoquy

Comment

http://www.cogsci.soton.ac.uk/cgi/psyc/newpsy

Check out one of the oldest, refereed, international, interdisciplinary electronic journals. This pioneer publication features a spectrum of full-text, fascinating articles and some pretty technical ones on an expanse of psychology-related topics.

[American Psychological Association]

Schizophrenia

Comment

http://www.schizophrenia.com/

The "Schizophrenia Information for Students" section includes a lengthy listing of links and resources for understanding all aspects of schizophrenia. Students and teachers can experience a great learning opportunity by reading messages posted in the "General Discussion Area" by individuals and families struggling with this disorder. A thoroughly informative, yet sensitive, Web site.

[The Schizophrenia Home Page]

Self & Psychology Magazine

Comment

http://www.cybertowers.com/selfhelp/

Written by mental health professionals, this online educational publication encourages discussion of psychology as applied to our daily lives. It hosts an excellent smorgasbord of practical, informative items, including a library of articles encompassing some 25 self-help topics, a comprehensive list of mental health listservs and newsgroups, and an amusing portfolio of "PsychToons" (cartoons related to psychology). A few choice articles:

> Precompetition Routines in Sport by Timothy M. Suchan
> Date/Acquaintance Rape Prevention for Him and Her by Connie Saindon
> Meditation: Try it out! by Marianne Ross, Ph.D.
> Easy Prey—The Ignorance of Youth; My Story, Part One by Cathy S.
> Virtual Meditation, a photo slide show

[Pioneer Development Resources, Inc.]

Comment	### Sensation and Perception Tutorials http://psych.hanover.edu/Krantz/sen_tut.html A few interesting self-paced lessons are assembled here. Though the selection is limited, more are promised. Probably worth checking back for late arrivals. [John H. Krantz, Ph.D, Hanover College Psychology Department]
Comment	### Shufflebrain http://www.indiana.edu/~pietsch/home.html#contents Key question is: "How does the brain store the mind?" A variety of articles and links, some scholarly, some wacky, are built into this master file. Just a few selections from the menu: The Beast's IQ Hologramic Mind Brain Swapping Split Human Brain Musical Brain Optics of Memory THUMPER: Can the brain think without its head? Head Transplant—are two heads better than one? The Human Corpus Callosum Music Therapy in Brain Damage [Paul Pietsch, Indiana University]
Comment	### Sigmund Freud and the Freud Archives http://plaza.interport.net/nypsan/freudarc.html This treasury of Internet resources related to Sigmund Freud and his work includes connections to museums, libraries, and biographies. [New York Psychoanalytic Institute]
Comment	### Skeptics Dictionary http://wheel.ucdavis.edu/%7Ebtcarrol/skeptic/dictcont.html Critical essays challenge the claims and suppositions of parapsychology, psychic phenomena, the occult, and pseudoscience. The site includes a comprehensive alphabetical index which encompasses everything from alien abductions, firewalking, and graphology, to zombies. [Robert Todd Carroll]

Comment	**Society for the Teaching of Psychology** http://spsp.clarion.edu/Division2/d2.html Subscribe to this electronic discussion network TIPS (Teaching in Psychological Sciences) to exchange teaching ideas with other psychology teachers. Perform quick keyword searches of past issues of the journal *Teaching of Psychology* or browse the easy-to-use index. A must-see site for all psychology teachers. [American Psychological Association]
Comment	**Stress Free Net** http://www.stressfree.com/ Though devoted to the reduction of stress, anxiety, and psychological and emotional pain, this is clearly a commercial enterprise, teasing with helpful information but also promoting the sponsor's services (at $100 per half hour consultation). Hum... The freebies are worth a peek, but the commercialism is a bit blatant. [Dr. Tony Rutner]
Comment	**Stress Space** http://www.glen-net.ca/sam/stress/ A schematic for constructing an inexpensive stress monitor, which may also be purchased ready-made, is included in the site. The fine list of references is worth a peek, and the "Laugh it off" section catalogs some amusing stories for a few free chuckles. [Stress Space]
Comment	**Study Skills** http://128.32.89.153/CalRENHP.html How can students overcome procrastination? This is but one topic addressed in this Web site, which provides practical tips and strategies for improving study skills. Brief tutorials on topics such as: When to Study, Learning by Listening, Effective-Notetaking, and Taking Essay Tests. [Pete Alvarez, Jr., Student Learning Center, University of California, Berkeley]

Comment	**Teaching Clinical Psychology** http://www1.rider.edu/~suler/tcp.html Though created for college psychology teachers, there is plenty of excellent content here to merit a visit. A large selection of course syllabi, student exercises, essays, and class handouts are stored in this well-organized virtual clearinghouse. Be sure to provide appropriate credits for any materials used. [J. Suler, Department of Psychology at Rider University]

A+

Comment	**Teaching of Psychology in Secondary Schools** http://spsp.clarion.edu/topss/topss.htm Over 800,000 students are enrolled annually in high school psychology classes. This American Psychological Association-sponsored clearinghouse was designed by and for high school psychology teachers to assure that these courses are of the highest caliber. TOPSS encourages a scientific approach to the teaching of high school psychology courses. Teachers can join this organization for a modest $25 fee. Be sure to check out the "Classroom Experiments/Labs/Demonstrations" section for several excellent instructional activities. The site includes a complete listing of relevant films and videos arranged by topic areas. An extensive listing of psychology textbooks and information on psychology clubs, psychology fairs, and student contests and scholarships should prove of interest. Currently, seven in-depth unit lesson plans (ranging from 25 to 56 pages each) are available through TOPSS. Descriptions of the plans are included on the Web page, but the complete unit is available only via regular mail. [American Psychological Association]

A+

Comment	**Teaching Psychology** http://psych.hanover.edu/APS/teaching.html Probably the best starting point for any psychology teacher. This Web page includes links to a broad array of Internet resources related to teaching psychology. Includes connections to college psychology courses and tutorials. [American Psychological Society]

Comment	**Theories of Child Development**
	http://207.86.133.69/children/index1.htm
	This basic introduction to the classical child development theories of Erikson, Mahler, and Freud includes concise descriptions of their individual theories related to the predictable phases of development from birth through adolescence.
	[Linda Chapman]
Comment	**USA Today Mental Health**
	http://www.usatoday.com/life/health/mentalh/lhmhe000.htm
	The national daily newspaper provides an indexed archive of articles on various aspects of mental health. Past issues have included items on eating disorders, depression, learning, neurological disorders, schizophrenia, shock treatment therapy, and suicide.
	[*USA Today*]
Comment	*Visual Illusions Gallery*
	http://aspen.uml.edu/~landrigad/ILLUSION.HTML
	This fun assortment of visual illusions should prove helpful in discussing sensation, perception, or neuroanatomy.
	[Dave Landrigan, Psychology Department, University of Massachusetts Lowell]
Comment	*Web of Addictions*
	http://www.well.com/user/woa/
	Teachers or students will find much useful information on the various forms of addiction, their treatment, and prevention. Links are provided to a variety of related fact sheets. An excellent rolodex provides addresses and phone numbers for contacting a large number of relevant organizations.
	[Andrew L. Homer and Dick Dillon]

Electronic Mailing Lists: Psychology

Many electronic mailing lists focus on topics of interest to psychology teachers and students. It is easy to subscribe. For example, to subscribe to the mailing list on Southern United States Culture:

Send an e-mail message to: LISTPROC@KNUTH.MTSU.EDU

Usually it is best to leave the "Subject" line blank. If your e-mail software requires something in the subject line, simply type a period.

Enter the message: subscribe BUBBA-L John Doe

Remember to enter your name instead of John Doe.

The format for the message is: subscribe <List_Name> <Your_Full_Name>

Aggression-Psychology
Psychological discussions of aggression
E-mail to: LISTSERV@MAELSTROM.ST.JOHNS.EDU

Anx-Dis
Professional forum on anxiety disorders
E-mail to: LISTSERV@MAELSTROM.ST.JOHNS.EDU

Anxiety-L
Support group for persons experiencing extreme anxiety
E-mail to: LISTPROC@FRANK.MTSU.EDU

C-Psych
Cross-cultural psychology
E-mail to: LISTSERV@MAELSTROM.ST.JOHNS.EDU

Cogsci
Forum on cognitive psychology
E-mail to: LISTSERV@NIC.SURFNET.NL

Commpsy
Study of community psychology
E-mail to: LISTSERV@MAELSTROM.ST.JOHNS.EDU

Counpsy
Counseling psychology practice and issues
E-mail to: LISTSERV@UGA.CC.EDU

Cybermind
Psychology of Cyberspace
E-mail to: LISTSERV@LISTSERV.AOL.COM

Debono
Forum on Edward de Bono's work on lateral thinking and creativity
E-mail to: LISTSERV@SJUVM.STJOHNS.EDU

Depress
Support for persons suffering depression
E-mail to: LISTSERV@SOUNDPRINT.BRANDYWINE.AMERICAN.EDU

Drugabus
Drug abuse forum
E-mail to: LISTSERV@UMAB.UMD.EDU

Familysci
Family issues
E-mail to: LISTSERV@UKCC.UKY.EDU

Gender
Study of gender and communication
E-mail: LISTSERV@VM.ITS.RPI.EDU

Group-L
Forum for discussion of group-related topics
E-mail to: GROUP-L-REQUEST@LISTS.BEST.COM

Interper
Interpersonal and small group communication
E-mail to: LISTSERV@VM.ITS.RPI.EDU

Ioob-L
Industrial psychology
E-mail to: LISTSERV@UGA.CC.UGA.EDU

Methods
Social science research methodologies
E-mail to: COMSERVE@VM.ITS.RPI.EDU

Powr-L
Psychology of women
E-mail to: LISTSERV@URIACC.URI.EDU

Psi-L
Discussion of parapsychology
E-mail to: LISTSERV@VM.ITS.RPI.EDU

Psycc-L
Community college psychology teachers forum
E-mail to: LISTSERV@UAFSYSB.UARK.EDU

Psy-Club
Psi Chi psychology honorary
E-mail to: LISTSERV@TC.UMN.EDU

Psy-Lang
Psychology of language
E-mail to: LISTSERV@MAELSTROM.ST.JOHNS.EDU

Psy-Media
Mental health in the media
E-mail to: MAJORDOMO@LISP.APA.ORG

Psych-Ci
Current issues in psychology
E-mail to: LISTSERV@MAELSTROM.ST.JOHNS.EDU

Psych-Type
Discussion of Myers-Briggs personality types
E-mail to: MAJORDOMO@SACAM.OREN.ORTN.EDU

Psycholoquy
Psycholoquy journal for general discussion of psychology
E-mail to: LISTSERV@PUCC.PRINCETON.EDU

Pwinet-L
Psychology of women forum
E-mail to: PSYCWOMEN-REQUEST@FRE.FSU.UMD.EDU

Self-L
Forum on self-esteem
E-mail to: LISTSERV@SOUNDPRINT.BRANDYWINE.AMERICAN.EDU

Smoke-Free
Support for those seeking to stop smoking
E-mail to: LISTSERV@RA.MSSTATE.EDU

Socpsy-L
Social psychology forum
E-mail to: LISTSERV@UGA.CC.UGA.EDU

Sportpsy
Sports psychology forum
E-mail to: LISTSERV%TEMPLEVM.BITNET@LISTSERV.NET

Traumatic-Stress
Discussion of traumatic stress
E-mail to: MAJORDOMO@FREUD.APA.ORG

Newsgroups: Psychology

alt.hypnosis	Hypnosis
alt.psychology.adlerian	Alfred Adler's life and theories
alt.psychology.help	General self-help discussion
alt.psychology.jung	Discussion of Carl Jung's ideas
alt.psychology.mistake-theory	Interesting discussion of mistakes
alt.psychology.nlp	Neuro-linguistic programming
alt.psychology.personality	Personality research and theories
alt.self-improve	Self-improvement suggestions
alt.sigma2.height	Exceptionally tall or short people
alt.society.mental-health	Mental health issues & malpractice
alt.support.anxiety-panic	Anxiety and panic disorders
alt.support.depression.manic	Manic depressive & bipolar disorders
alt.support.depression	Persons experiencing depression & mood disorders
alt.recovery	General discussion of recovery
alt.recovery.aa	Alcoholics Anonymous
alt.recovery.na	Narcotics Anonymous
alt.recovery.compulsive-eat	Compulsive eating disorders
alt.recovery.nicotine	Support for persons quitting nicotine
alt.recovery.panic-anxiety .self-help	Cognitive treatment of anxiety and panic disorders
alt.recovery.procrastinate	Support for procrastinators
alt.sexual.abuse.recovery	Aiding recovery from sexual abuse trauma
alt.support.dissociation	Dissociative disorders; multiple personality disorder
alt.support.eating-disord	Eating disorders
alt.support.epilepsy	For persons experiencing epilepsy and their families
alt.support.grief	For persons experiencing grief and loss
alt.support.learning-disab	For persons with learning disabilities

Newsgroups: Psychology (Continued)

alt.support.loneliness	For those experiencing loneliness
alt.support.ocdΩObsessive	Compulsive disorder self-help group
alt.support.opp-defiant	For those experiencing oppositional defiant disorder
alt.support.personality	For those with personality disorders
alt.support.schizophrenia	Schizophrenia support group
bit.listserv.autism	Autism
bit.listserv.deaf-L	Deafness
bit.listserv.down-syn	Down syndrome
bit.listserv.ioob-L	Industrial psychology
bit.listserv.psycgrad	Psychology graduate students
bit.listserv.sportpsy	Exercise & sports psychology
k12.Ed.special	Students with special needs
misc.creativity	Discussions of the creative process
misc.kids	Child development and behavior
sci.cognitive	Study of perception, memory, judgment, and reasoning
sci.psychology.consciousness	Nature of consciousness (moderated)
sci.psychology.journals .psyche	E-journal on consciousness (moderated)
sci.psychology.misc	General discussion of psychology
sci.psychology.personality	Study of personality
sci.psychology.psyche	PSYCHE, a journal on consciousness (moderated)
sci.psychology.psycoloquy	Psycoloquy, a refereed psychology journal.
sci.psychology.psychotherapy	Psychotherapy and counseling practice
sci.psychology.research	Moderated discussion of psychology research
sci.psychology.theory	Psychological theories
soc.support.depression.crisis	Support for persons experiencing crises

Newsgroups: Psychology (Continued)

soc.support.depression.family	For families of depressed individuals
soc.support.depression.manic	Bipolar/manic depression
soc.support.depression.misc	Depression and mood disorders
soc.support.depression.seasonal	Seasonal affective disorder
soc.support.depression.treatment	Assorted treatments for depression
soc.support.loneliness	Moderated discussion of loneliness

Section 8

GEOGRAPHY

Best Web Sites: Geography

Comment

Adventure Online

http://www.adventureonline.com/index.html

A series of distance-learning expeditions which have employed interactive software and real-time telecommunications to follow the progress of educator/adventurers through several exciting and interest-holding expeditions. Archives of past trips are available for teachers and students. Each adventure includes appropriate teaching resources. Examples of past projects:

Project Central America was a two-month, 1,900-mile learning expedition sponsored by Minnetonka Public Schools and the Bush Educational Leaders Program. Although the adventure was completed in 1994, the resource materials are all accessible at this Web site. Teachers can download an activity file with suggested lessons in the art, history, geography, religion, and language of Central America. Colorful maps and photographs permit the students to follow the adventurers' progress.

Running the Nile, the first kayak descent of Victoria Nile in Uganda, Africa, was completed in early 1996. Real-time Internet-posted reports recorded the progress of the adventurers. To help teachers connect lessons on Africa with the online adventure, a teacher resource file included:

    Journal Updates from the Team in Africa
    Water Quality, Topography, and Life Science Data from the
    Nile River
    Lesson Plans and Classroom Activities
    Photos, Tips & Templates for Multi-Media Presentations
    Other Resources for the Nile Classroom
    Ask the Online Expert

Magellan Global Adventure and *Trindade Now 96* formed the first e-sail adventure as the Schurmann family crew visited exotic places en route to re-creating Ferdinand Magellan's circumnavigation of the world. Satellite transmission of video clips put student adventurers at the helm of this exciting expedition.

International Greenland Expedition. In May of 1997, a similar expedition was undertaken to circumnavigate Greenland. Connect to Adventure Online home page to stay informed of future expeditions.

[Event Media]

Comment	**Alternative Fuels Data Center**
	http://www.afdc.doe.gov/
	An extensive collection of documents on alternative fuels. Research reports and legislation related to use of alternative fuels in transportation are most likely to be of interest to teachers.
	[National Renewable Energy Laboratory]
Comment	**American Rivers**
	http://www.igc.apc.org/amrivers/
	This site is dedicated to protecting and restoring America's river systems. The backlist of press releases is particularly noteworthy.
	[American Rivers, national conservation organization]
Comment	**Antarctica: A Resource for Teachers and Students**
	http://www.icair.iac.org.nz/education/resource/homepage/homepage.htm
	Beautiful pictures, interactive learning activities, and links to virtually anything related to the study of the Antarctic can be found here. Vast resources in the following categories: Antarctica: That Last Great Wilderness Information about Antarctica Other Antarctic Resources Studying the Antarctic Student Self-Study Units Linking Education with Antarctic Research in New Zealand Where Do I Go for More Information about the Antarctic? Bibliography Glossary
Comment	**Arid Lands Newsletter**
	http://ag.arizona.edu/OALS/ALN/ALNHome.html
	A first-rate site filled with beautiful photographs and well-written articles about all aspects of deserts.
	[Office of Arid Land Studies, University of Arizona]

Comment	**Atlapedia Online** http://www.atlapedia.com/index.html This electronic hybrid of an atlas and encyclopedia provides basic information about the geography, religion, climate, people, history, language, and economy of the world's countries. As with all sites, be sure to read the sponsor's copyright restrictions on fair use. [Latimer Clarke Corporation]
Comment	**A Brief Guide to State Facts** http://www.ecnet.net/users/gdlevin/sstudies.html Which state has the motto "The welfare of the people shall be the supreme law"? What is the official state bird of Nevada? This site offers a quick reference to basic facts about the 50 states. [Holly Sittel]
Comment	**Bureau of Land Management Environmental Education Homepage** http://www.blm.gov/education/education.html A jackpot of teacher resources on topics such as gold mining, fire, Great Basin ecosystems, noxious weeds, and riparian areas. A very useful collection of teaching materials on environmental education. A few of the current items:

> Archaeology and History
>   Environmental Technology is an Ancient Science
>   Mystery of the Mesa
>   Project Archaeology
>   Public Lands and Your Students
>   Steel Rails and Iron Horses
>   Solving the Mystery of Santa Cruz
> Ecosystems
>   Alaska's Cold Desert
>   The Big Empty
>   Understanding Ecosystem Management
>   The High Plains: Land of Extremes
> Environmental Ethics
>   Leave No Trace
>   Cultural Ethics
>   Weeds
>   Wilderness
>   Anglers Code of Ethics

Tread Lightly Pledge
Hunter's Pledge
River Ethics
Wildflower Conservation
Back Country Byways
Wildlife Watching
Mountain Biking Ethics
Hiking/Backpacking

[Bureau of Land Management, U.S. Department of the Interior]

Canadian National Atlas

Comment

http://www-nais.ccm.emr.ca/schoolnet/

Several interesting and educational interactive learning activities about Canada and its geography. French version of the site is also available. A large collection of all kinds of maps can be accessed. Here is a sampling of the activities and resources available in this archive:

Make a Map
Interactive Geography Quiz
Canadian Issues
Our Home: Atlas of Canadian Communities
Defacto: Geographical Facts about Canada
Geographical Names
Hot Topics
Teaching Resources
Ask the Harkster

[Industry Canada; National Resources Canada]

Canadisk Online

Comment

http://schoolnet2.carleton.ca/cdisk/

Several materials for teaching about Canada are included in both English and French versions. A sampling of lesson plans and class projects:

Canada and the Space Shuttle
Canada Unity Conference
Cruise the News
Current Event Jeopardy
Data Gathering, World War II
Exploring Our Roots
Geography & Current Events
Great Lakes & St. Lawrence
History of Local Community
Immigrant Ancestors

Interviewing Historical Figures
Making a Cartogram
Oral History, Team Approach
Oral Reports, Personality Bags
People, Places, and Events
Relationships with Older People
Sequencing of Events

[SchoolNet Support Group]

Cartography

Comment   http://baby.indstate.edu:80/gga/gga_cart/index.html

A good collection of materials on the craft of mapmaking. Overuse of glitzy graphics on the home page significantly slows load-time. Topics included in this Web site:

Introduction to Cartography
Cartographic Examples
University Sites
Map Related Government Sites
Map Related Libraries
Map Related Commercial Sites
Mapping Software Vendors
Interactive Graphics
Maps*Maps*Maps
Special Maps

[Department of Geography, Indiana State University]

Celebrating a Lifetime of Conservation: John Muir

Comment   http://ice.ucdavis.edu/John_Muir/John_Muir_Day_
Study_Guide/

John Muir, scientist, explorer, and environmental advocate, is credited as the founder of the conservation movement. Environmental education activities, organized by grade level, are available in this site named in honor of the pioneer conservationist.

C.I.A. World Fact Book

Comment   http://www.odci.gov/cia/publications/nsolo/wfb-all.htm

Updated annually, this massive reference covering all the countries of the world is now available online. Extensive coverage for each country includes information on its economy, government, people, geography, defense, communication, and transportation. An extensive collection of downloadable maps is included in the site. If the hardback edition is not on your desk, bookmark this page or download the whole volume onto your hard drive.

[Central Intelligence Agency]

Comment

Connections+: Geography Lesson Plans

http://www.mcrel.org/connect/plus/latlong.html

This no frills, small collection of teacher-made geography lessons assembled from various sources is worth a peek.

[McREL, U.S. Department of Education]

Comment

Coordinate Systems

http://www.utexas.edu/depts/grg/gcraft/notes/coordsys/coordsys.html

A superb overview of coordinate systems for georeferencing. Clear graphics illustrate the complete range of coordinate systems employed in navigation, mapping, and positioning.

[Department of Geography, The University of Texas at Austin]

Comment

Country Studies

http://lcweb2.loc.gov/frd/cs/cshome.html

An interdisciplinary team of experts analyzes the economic, social, political, and national security institutions of the 70 countries, providing extensive background information on each.

[Library of Congress]

Comment

County Outline Maps

http://www.lib.utexas.edu/Libs/PCL/Map_collection/county_outline.html

A complete collection of county outline maps for all fifty states. The lean, precise, downloadable maps were created by the U.S. Census Bureau.

[Perry-Castañeda Library Map Collection, The University of Texas at Austin]

Comment	**Earth Foundation** http://www.earthfound.com/ This private foundation seeks to educate students on major environmental issues and to muster schools into action to raise funds for conservation. Probably the most useful feature for teachers is "Eco-News," which provides updates on threats to the environment. [Earth Foundation]
Comment	**Edu-Source: Resources for Environmental Education** http://edu-source.com/masthead.html The home page graphics alone make this site worth visiting. Though clearly a commercial site, selling posters and graphic design services, you can access an excellent lesson on the geology of the Grand Canyon and download free clip art (mostly images of the Southwest and wildlife). [Design & Sales, Incorporated]
Comment	**Electronic Field Trips** http://www.pbs.org/insidepbs/learningservices/eft.html Hundreds of social studies classes have participated in several very successful electronic field trips during the past couple of years. Scientists and other experts report the progress of exciting expeditions with daily Internet updates. These learning events provide a rich glimpse of the Internet's instructional potential. Information about participating in these exemplary, interactive learning experiences can be found at this site. Among the successful ventures thus far: Pyramids—The Inside Story Live from Antarctica Wild Wings Heading South Order in the Court: Juvenile Justice in the Eighteenth Century Three Men and a Balloon Live from Mars: Countdown Ice Mummies of the Inca Everest Quest Live from the Hubble Space Telescope Science in the Rainforest Conflict Resolution in the Global Village [Public Broadcasting System]

Comment	**Department of Energy**
	http://www.doe.gov/
	Pretty dull, uninspiring site, but there is a ton of technical information available here. You'll have to dig for the gems. It could use some technical help with its Web design. The "D.O.E. Fact Sheets" are worth exploring.
	[United States Department of Energy]
Comment	**Energy & Environment**
	http://zebu.uoregon.edu/energy.html
	Global warming and ozone depletion are two of the environmental issues addressed in this clearinghouse. A variety of energy/environment-related links lead teachers and students to some of the most up-to-date information.
	[The Electronic Universe Project]
Comment	**Envirolink**
	http://envirolink.org/
	Started in 1991 by a Carnegie Mellon University freshman, this nonprofit organization bills itself as "the world's largest online environmental information clearinghouse." Such a massive depository of information would be overwhelming if it were not so well organized. While the volume of content included in this site is impressive, it is exceeded by the beauty of its Web page design. The superior, crisp graphic design makes this one of the most visually attractive sites on the Internet. Don't miss it!
	[The EnviroLink Network]
Comment	**Environmental Education**
	http://www.nceet.snre.umich.edu/
	This excellent collection of classroom resources offers lesson plans, Earth Day activities, fact sheets, data files, guides, and catalogs. The site also includes a listing of environmental workshops and conferences, organizations, employment opportunities, and professional development events. The Environmental Data/Facts/Statistics page includes a great selection of data that might be used to design lessons or student projects.
	[National Consortium for Environmental Education and Training]

A+

	Environmental Protection Agency
Comment	http://www.epa.gov/
	A convenient depository of environment-related teaching aids. A small sampling:
	Chesapeake Bay: Introduction to an Ecosystem Environmental Careers Resource Guide Environmental Education (and having fun at the same time) Guide to Environmental Issues Hazardous Waste (Superfund) Haz-Ed: Classroom Activities for Understanding Hazardous Waste Turning the Tide on Trash: A Learning Guide on Marine Debris Acid Rain—Student Resources Ozone Depletion Setting the Record Straight: Secondhand Smoke Is a Preventable Health Risk What Is Acid Rain?
	[U.S. Environmental Protection Agency]
	Exploring the Environment
Comment	http://www.cotf.edu/ETE/
	As part of NASA's High Performance Computing and Communications program, this site focuses upon cooperative learning activities to promote "problem-based learning" and encourage students to ask the right questions, more than generate the right answers. Learning modules lead students through simulations, such as tracking a hurricane, monitoring water quality, and grappling with survival of the Amazon rain forest.
	[National Aeronautical and Space Administration]
	Finding Your Way with Map and Compass
Comment	http://info.er.usgs.gov/fact-sheets/finding-your-way/finding-your-way.html
	This superb tutorial on finding your way with a topographical map and compass includes excellent graphic images.
	[U.S. Geological Survey]

Comment	*GeoCities* http://www.geocities.com/BHI/geoviewer.html Enter the street address, city, state, and ZIP code of virtually any location in the United States; GeoCities will generate a map. You can even sign up for a free personal home page or a free e-mail account through this very impressive site. [GeoCity Company]
Comment	*Geographers Craft* http://www.utexas.edu/depts/grg/gcraft/contents.html This award-winning site features an exceptional collection of college course materials on geographical research techniques. While some of the content may be too advanced for most high school students, teachers will find much they can incorporate into their courses. The lecture and discussion notes, warm-up exercises, and sample test and study questions are worth examining. Previous semesters' final class projects are posted as valuable models of active teaching with practical application of the course content. [Department of Geography, University of Texas at Austin]
Comment	*Geography Lesson Plans* http://www.eduplace.com/ss/autoact/ss_1.html Young students learn geography by plotting the cities of their favorite sports teams. This is just one of the lesson ideas this book publisher has assembled in a splendid collection of geography lesson plans for K-6 students. [Houghton Mifflin Company]
Comment	*Geography Teaching Resources* http://wwwhost.cc.utexas.edu/ftp/pub/grg/virtdept/contents.html Links are provided to over 100 online sources for geography instructional materials. A few of the topic categories include: Cartography and Map Interpretation Cultural Geography Earth's Environment and Society Geographic Information Systems Human Geography Introduction to Geography

Physical Geography
Regional & Area Studies
Urban & Economic Geography
Virtual Fieldtrips

[University of Texas, Austin]

GeoNet Game

Comment

http://www.hmco.com/hmco/school/geo/indexlo.html

GeoNet Game, a geography game based on the national geography standards, offers two levels of difficulty to permit students as young as fourth grade to answer relevant questions. While the graphics are a bit disappointing for a commercial site, the variety of geography questions makes this a useful motivational tool.

[Houghton Mifflin Company]

GeoPedia

Comment

http://www.geopedia.com/

Information on every country in the world can be found in this colorful resource. Individual country profiles include data on "geography, climate, people, religion, language, history and economy making." Materials and software from the site may be downloaded and used for educational purposes. Check out the "Legal Notice" button on the home page.

[Latimer Clarke Corporation]

Green & Growing: From the Ground Up

Comment

http://www.GateWest.net/~green/

This online lesson guide on agriculture, food, and sustainable development is divided into five units:

The History of Agriculture and a Description of Sustainable Development
Soil
Agriculture and Chemicals
The Real Cost of Food
Everything's Connected

Teachers may access lessons, background essays, and worksheets for in-class use. The "Complete Teachers' Guide" can be downloaded, though it is a pretty large document.

[Green & Growing, Bryan Johnson and Keith Turner]

Comment	## Groundwater Education http://gwrp.cciw.ca/education/index.html Nothing fancy, but a good basic introduction to the problem of groundwater quality. Featured content: Groundwater fact sheet Basic groundwater information Groundwater quiz A test of your groundwater knowledge Interactive modeling of leachate migration from a landfill Experiment with an actual groundwater model [Groundwater Remediation Project of the National Water Research Institute of Environment Canada]
Comment	## Helping Your Child Learn Geography http://www.ed.gov/pubs/parents/Geography/ Although designed for parents, many of the ideas at this site could be adapted by teachers. Pass a few of the ideas along to the parents of your students for their reinforcement of your class content. A selection of free and inexpensive materials is also offered. [Office of Educational Research and Improvement, U.S. Department of Education]
Comment	## How Far Is It? http://www.indo.com/distance/ Enter two cities anywhere in the world and this server will calculate the longitude and latitude of both places and display the distance between them (as the crow flies). The site can link to the Xerox PARC Map Server to generate a map showing the two places. [Jakarta's Department of Tourism, Bali Online]
Comment	## How to Use a Compass http://www.uio.no/~kjetikj/compass/ This illustrated tutorial can be printed and used for classroom purposes as long as the author is credited. [Kjetil Kjernsmos]

A+

Comment

Jason Project

http://www.jason.org/

Wow! What a great way to teach geography! Each year, the Jason Project undertakes a two-week scientific exploration in a remote area of the world. Live, interactive Internet broadcasts permit students around the world to follow the progress of the expedition. Previous years' online projects have included Journey from the Center of the Earth, Field Study: Bird Populations, Aquatic Field Study, and Novel Talks. Videotapes and curriculum materials from past expeditions are available for purchase.

An excellent set of lessons, activities, and downloadable maps enables teachers to facilitate the learning process. The "Teacher Forum" is a discussion group permitting teachers to exchange instructional ideas about the Jason Projects. The Web pages are very professionally done with eye-pleasing, but rapidly loading, graphics.

[Dr. Robert D. Ballard, The JASON Foundation for Education]

Comment

Journey Exchange Project

http://www.csnet.net/minds-eye/journey/

"Students from grades 3-12 communicate a planned and researched five-day journey across the world into another student's mind using geographic, social, economic, political, and historical clues." Students cooperate in researching, creating, and organizing a multimedia trip portfolio containing clues. They exchange portfolios and attempt to discover the path of the proposed journey. Inviting, colorful graphics illustrate this creative Web site.

[Brian Maguire, Community School Networks]

Comment

K-12 Electronic Guide for African Resources on the Internet

http://www.sas.upenn.edu/African_Studies/Home_Page/
AFR_GIDE.html

Great jumping-off point for locating information about Africa. Dozens of sites contain resources arranged in the following topical areas:

K-12 Information
Country-Specific Information
The Multimedia Archive
Africa in the Library
Languages of Africa
Environment in Africa
Travel in Africa
African American Resources

[Ali B. Dinar, African Studies Program, U. of Pennsylvania]

Comment

Latest Earthquake Information

http://quake.wr.usgs.gov/QUAKES/CURRENT/current.html

Current updates on earthquakes anywhere in the world, and additional information on studying earthquakes, hazards, and preparedness are featured in this official government site.

[U.S. Geological Survey]

Comment

Living Planet Campaign

http://www.livingplanet.org/action/

This environmental activist's Web site is dedicated to preserving endangered species by changing human behavior.

[The World Wide Fund For Nature]

A+

Comment

Map Machine

http://www.nationalgeographic.com/ngs/maps/cartographic.html

The best of the best. Consistent with the perennially high standards of the National Geographic Society, this informative, eye-catching site provides an interactive world atlas with in-depth information about each country. The only downside: some parts only work if your browser is equipped with advanced plug-ins.

[National Geographic Society]

Comment

Mapmaker, Mapmaker, Make Me a Map

http://loki.ur.utk.edu/ut2Kids/maps/map.html

This introductory hypertext tutorial on mapmaking provides a self-paced learning experience. The "Mapmaker Crossword

Puzzle" can be printed by the teacher and used as a cooperative class activity.

[Office of University Relations, The University of Tennessee]

_A+_

MayaQuest

Comment

http://www.mecc.com/mayaquest.html

This top-notch site represents the outstanding educational potential of the Internet. Annually, since 1995, MayaQuest teams have completed totally kid-directed expeditions. The three-month expeditions explore the Mayan world of Mexico and Central America. A team of explorer/cyclists interacts with students across the world via laptop computers and satellite equipment, permitting students to determine the course of the expedition by submitting e-mail votes. Students interact with the explorers and archaeologists at real archaeological sites, exchanging questions and responses with the researchers. Full participation requires purchase of a $95 classroom kit, though this is a valuable learning resource even if the kit is not purchased.

[Earth Treks, Inc.]

National Council for Geographic Education

Comment

http://multimedia2.freac.fsu.edu/ncge/

The N.C.G.E. provides a variety of programs, awards, and publications to promote geographic education. Membership information is available at its home page.

[National Council for Geographic Education]

National Geographic

Comment

http://www.nationalgeographic.com/main.html

This online edition maintains the exemplary standards of its print edition with its splendid interviews, essays, and photographs. One of the most valuable features is an index of National Geographic Society publications, including _National Geographic_ magazine since 1888. Be sure to check out its collection of lessons and activities, organized by grade level. Lessons currently available:

> A Summer Day
> Environmental Explorer

Neighborhood Services—Where Are They and Why?
Story Maps
Fighting Cholera With Maps
Look! You're Wearing Geography
Regions: A Hands-on Approach
What's Your Region Really Like?
Made in the U.S.A.
Mental Mapping

[National Geographic Society]

National Renewable Energy Laboratory

Comment

http://www.nrel.gov/

This attractive Web site presents valuable information on the technology of energy from the sun, wind, earth's heat, plants. Many excellent, nontechnical fact sheets are available for online viewing or to be downloaded. Be sure to check out the informative section on "energy solutions for consumers." The generous use of colorful, creative graphics does slow load-time of some pages.

[U.S. Department of Energy]

Perry-Castañeda Library Map Collection

Comment

http://www.lib.utexas.edu/Libs/PCL/Map_collection/Map_collection.html

An exceptional depository of approximately 2,000 public domain electronic maps, including over 300 of the United States. All can be downloaded. Most are in JPEG or GIF formats, usually around 200K; however, some are very large.

[The University of Texas at Austin]

Pollution Prevention Northwest Newsletter

Comment

http://pprc.pnl.gov:80/pprc/pubs/newslets/newslett.html

A bimonthly newsletter provides valuable information on strategies, research reports, and other important issues of pollution prevention.

[Pacific Northwest Pollution Prevention Resource Center]

Project GeoSim

Comment

http://geosim.cs.vt.edu/index.html

A set of multimedia, instructional geography modules provides an introductory tutorial program and a laboratory simulation for each lesson. The supporting computer software for each module is available via FTP in a variety of formats. Currently Available Project GeoSim Modules:

> Human Population (HumPop) and International Population (IntlPop)
> Migration Modeling (MigModel)
> Mental Maps (MMap)
> Congressional Apportionment (MigPol)
> Sense of Place (SnsPlace)

[Departments of Computer Science and Geography at Virginia Tech]

Comment

Rare Map Collection

http://scarlett.libs.uga.edu/darchive/hargrett/maps/colamer.html

Access an exquisite collection of old and rare maps. Samples:

> Florida et regiones vicinae (1625)
> Virginiae item et Floridae Americae Provinciarum nova descriptio (1633])
> New description of Carolina (1676)
> Louisiana and the River Mississippi (1721)
> Southeastern North America (First appearance of "Georgia"—1732)
> British American plantations (1754)
> The Cherokee Nation (1760)

Comment

Remote Sensing Project

http://www.oneonta.edu/~baumanpr/ncge/rstf.htm

This Project encourages the understanding of the Earth's landscape through the use of aerial or satellite images. A few JPEG-format images are available for viewing.

[National Council for Geographic Education]

Comment

Right to Know Network

http://rtk.net/

Users who register for free accounts can access massive data banks on issues related to the environment and housing.

[OMB Watch and The Unison Institute, non-profit organizations]

Comment	**RotWeb** http://net.indra.com/~topsoil/Compost_Menu.html A complete guide to composting, this teacher resource file includes a list of schools undertaking composting demonstration projects welcoming visitors. A text-only version is also available. [Eric S. Johnson]
Comment	**San Diego Earth Times** http://www.sdearthtimes.com/ This monthly electronic magazine presents an array of environmental topics, a monthly Calendar of Earth Friendly Events, the Marketplace, Organic Gardening Tips, Eco-puzzles, book reviews, and an archive of back issues. Well organized layout and enriching, not overpowering, graphics complement the content. [San Diego Earth Times]
Comment	**Sense of Place** http://geosim.cs.vt.edu/snsplace.html Download a computer simulation which "combines a comprehensive statistical database with a set of simple visualization techniques to allow students to gain an understanding of the characteristics of U.S. counties. Students can examine data for any one of the statistical variables in the database....Symbolic mapping is used to illustrate spatial characteristics of a state or county, such as its size, shape, and location, as well as regional patterns among different counties." The software is available in Macintosh (System 7.0+), MS-DOS, and MS Windows formats. [Project GeoSim, Department of Computer Science, Virginia Tech]
Comment	**Solstice** http://solstice.crest.org/ Check this site for just about anything and everything related to energy efficiency and renewable energy (solar, wind, geothermal). Nothing fancy; easy-to-use. Not loaded down with unnecessary, time-consuming graphics.

[The Center for Renewable Energy and Sustainable Technology, Project of the Solar Energy Research and Education Foundation]

Statistical Abstract of the United States

Comment

http://www.medaccess.com/census/census_s.htm

View more than 1,400 charts and tables compiled from the 1994 U.S. census. A large, easy-to-use database provides many opportunities for instructional activities and student research projects.

A sample of the content areas:

> Agriculture
> Construction and Housing
> Education
> Energy
> Geography and Environment
> Health and Nutrition
> Income, Expenditures, and Wealth
> Labor Force, Employment, and Earnings
> Law Enforcement, Courts, and Prisons
> Natural Resources—Forestry, Fisheries, and Mining
> Parks, Recreation, and Travel
> Population

[MedAccess Corporation]

TerraQuest

Comment

http://www.terraquest.com/

This marvelous example of the educational potential of the Internet is perhaps the Web's most outstanding travel site. Using digital technology, photographs were processed in the field and loaded onto the TerraQuest Web page via satellite. Users can follow the day-to-day progress of their adventures. Three exceptional expeditions have been logged thus far: A climb up Yosemite National Park's "El Capitan," the beauty and wildlife of "Virtual Galápagos," and a polar exploration through "Virtual Antarctica." Don't miss this site!

[Mountain Travel-Sobek and WorldTravel Partners]

	Travelocity
Comment	http://www.travelocity.com/
	Undoubtedly the largest collection of travel information on the Internet. The site includes a guide to U.S. parks, daily weather alerts, in-depth travelogues, and hundreds of maps.
	[Worldview Systems, Rand McNally]
	Trip through the Grand Canyon
Comment	http://river.ihs.gov/GrandCanyon/GCrt.html
	Users take a trip through the Grand Canyon. Beautiful photographs and narrative text provide a glimpse of the beauty and thrill of the 240-mile canyon raft ride. Overflowing with information about the Grand Canyon. Very well done!
	[Leonard Thurman]
	U.S. Gazetteer
Comment	http://www.census.gov/cgi-bin/gazetteer
	Enter a city, town, or ZIP code to download geographical coordinates, a map, and additional information about the location. A great site for obtaining local maps.
	[U.S. Bureau of Census]
	U.S. Geological Survey
Comment	http://www.usgs.gov/
	One of the most attractive government-sponsored Web sites. The "learning resources" section contains excellent instructional resources on working with maps and understanding global change.
	[U.S. Geological Survey]
	Virtual Cave
Comment	http://www.goodearth.com/virtcave.html
	What is the difference between stalactites and stalagmites? Then what are stegamites? You'll see beautiful images of all three, plus much more, in this outstanding electronic cave tour. Take your students on a Cyber-spelunking field trip.
	[Djuna Bewley]

Comment	**Virtual Library: Environment** http://ecosys.drdr.virginia.edu/All.html Massive alphabetical listing of hundreds of environment-related resources available on the World Wide Web. Lots of chaff, but many gems are hidden among the listings. [University of Virginia]
Comment	**Virtual Town** http://wwwcsif.cs.ucdavis.edu/virt-town/welcome.html Access a gigantic Web directory by clicking buildings and other places on the virtual Town map. Activate the "Museum" hot spot and a list of excellent online museum exhibits appear. Separate text-based and graphics versions of the link are provided. The graphic one does contain a very large map, which can take a long time loading. The "Government" building leads to approximately two dozen federal government home pages, including the House of Representatives, Senate, White House, and Library of Congress. The "Virtual Town Travel Agency" uncovers a smattering of virtual tours in the U.S. and around the world. Not a great deal of original content is found here, but the novel map and building concept logically and efficiently organizes a virtual ton of information. [Vik Varma & Elaine Lazarte]
Comment	**Wind Energy Weekly** http://www.igc.apc.org/awea/ Teachers receive a free electronic subscription to this newspaper. The hardcopy, commercial subscription costs $595 a year! [American Wind Energy Association]
Comment	**Working With Maps** http://www.usgs.gov/education/learnweb/Maps.html Students master basic mapmaking and map-reading skills in a series of interdisciplinary lessons on mapping for grades 7-12. Location, navigation, information, and exploration comprise the lesson themes. Each lesson contains an introduction, two activities, and ready-to-photocopy student handouts. Most lessons are completed in two hours or used as a longer term project. [U.S. Geological Survey]

Comment	**World Wide Fund: Kids & Teachers Area** http://www.panda.org/kids/index.htm A small archive of environmental education activities includes lessons, fact sheets, and comic books on saving the world's endangered species. Updated regularly, so check back often. [World Wide Fund for Nature]
Comment	**WXP: The Weather Processor** http://wxp.atms.purdue.edu/ Use a special software package to visualize current and archived meteorological data. Clearly designed for the advanced user, over 600 graphic images (many quite large) are available. Some are updated hourly. [Department of Earth and Atmospheric Sciences, Purdue University]
Comment	**You Can: Acid Rain** http://www.nbn.com/youcan/acid/acid.html Basic explanation of acid rain with easy experiments for testing acidity of local rainfall. Colorful graphics. [Jok R. Church]

ELECTRONIC MAILING LISTS: GEOGRAPHY

Many electronic mailing lists focus on topics of interest to geography teachers and students. It is easy to subscribe. For example, to subscribe to the mailing list ASEH-L on environmental history:

Send an e-mail message to: LISTPROC@UNICORN.ACS.TTU.EDU

Usually it is best to leave the "Subject" line blank. If your e-mail software requires something in the subject line, simply type a period.

Enter the message: subscribe ASEH-L John Doe

Remember to enter your name instead of John Doe.

The format for the message is: subscribe <List_Name> <Your_Full_Name>

AAA-Environment-Related-Web-Sites
Information about environment-related Web sites
E-mail to: WEBSCOUT@WEBCOM.COM

Aridlands-NL
Newsletter covering all aspects of desert ecology
E-mail to: MAJORDOMO@AG.ARIZONA.EDU

Aseh-L
Environmental history forum
E-mail to: LISTPROC@UNICORN.ACS.TTU.EDU

Biosph-L
Interdisciplinary discussion of the earth's biosphere
E-mail to: LISTSERV@LISTSERV.AOL.COM

Ceres-L
Conservation of earth resources
E-mail to: LISTSERV@WVNVM.WVNET.EDU

Ecotoxicology
Environmental protection and restoration of damaged ecosystems
E-mail to: LISTSERV@LISTSERV.VT.EDU

Elan
Environment in Latin America forum
E-mail to: LISTSERV@CSF.COLORADO.EDU

Enviroethics
Environmental ethics discussion
E-mail to: MAILBASE@MAILBASE.AC.UK

Forsum
"Forest Summit Online" forum for teachers
E-mail to: LISTSERV@BROWNVM.BROWN.EDU

Geoged
Geography education forum
E-mail to: LISTSERV@UKCC.UKY.EDU

Geograph
Geography research forum
E-mail to: LISTSERV@SEARN.SUNET.SE

Geography
Geographers' forum
E-mail to: LISTSERV@SEARN.SUNET.SE

Geopol
Political Geography Network
E-mail to: LISTSERV@LSV.UKY.EDU

GRC
Geographic Resources Center forum
E-mail to: MAJORDOMO@GEOG.HKBU.EDU.HK

Infoterra
International forum on environmental topics
E-mail to: MAJORDOMO@CEDAR.UNIVIE.AC.AT

Ingrafx
Interdisciplinary forum on cartography
E-mail to: LISTSERV@UBVM.CC.BUFFALO.EDU

Natlit-L
Discussion of resources on cnvironmental education, environmental law, and resource management
E-mail to: LISTPROC@ENVIROLINK.ORG

Solar-Ll
Energy conservation and renewable energy efforts on Long Island
E-mail to: LISTPROC@IBIX.COM

Tap-Resources
Forum on management of publicly owned natural resources
E-mail to: LISTSERVER@ESSENTIAL.ORG

Urban-L
Urban planning forum
E-mail to: LISTSERV%TREARN.BITNET@VM1.NODAK.EDU

Urbanites
Self-sufficiency in everyday life
E-mail to: URBANITES-REQUEST@PSYCHE.MIT.EDU

Newsgroups: Geography

alt.disasters.earthquakes	Earthquakes
alt.save.the.earth	Ecological issues
bit.listserv.geograph	Geography in general
misc.transport.urban-transit	Urban transportation
rec.travel.africa	Travel tales and tips for Africa trips
rec.travel.asia	Go East, young man. All about getting to and around in Asia
rec.travel.australia+nz	Travel in Australia and New Zealand
rec.travel.europe	Travel throughout Europe
rec.travel.latin-america	Latin American travel
rec.travel.usa-canada	Travel in the United States and Canada
rec.outdoors.national-parks	Activities in the national parks
sci.environment	Discussions of ecological issues
sci.geo.earthquake	Everything about earthquakes
sci.geo.geology	Geology
sci.geo.meteorology	Everyone talks about the weather
sci.geo.oceanography	Tides, currents, cybersail the seven seas
sci.geo.rivers+lakes	Water, water, everywhere
talk.environment	Discussion among environmentalists

GOVERNMENT

Best Web Sites: Government

Comment	**All Politics** http://allpolitics.com/ This excellent interactive site features an outstanding selection of articles on major contemporary politics. You have the opportunity to exchange views on issues of the day, to participate in public opinion polls, or to view experts' interpretations of political events. [Cable News Network/Time]
Comment	**Almanac of American Politics** http://pn1.politicsnow.com/resource/almanac/index.htm This online version of "the definitive guide to the American political scene" is fully searchable for profiles of all the members of Congress and governors and for thoughtful analyses of the political scene. [National Journal, *PoliticsNow*]
Comment	**American Bar Association** http://www.abanet.org/ LawLink provides dozens of hotlinks to legislative, judicial, executive, and regulatory offices. Reports on actions and recommendations of the A.B.A. annual meetings are posted regularly. A very thorough search engine facilitates easy location of law-related topics. [American Bar Association]
Comment	**American Civil Liberties Union (ACLU)** http://www.aclu.org/ This nonpartisan, nonprofit organization is committed to protecting "the basic civil liberties of all Americans and extending them to groups that have traditionally been denied them." Its award-winning Web site shares a variety of resources related to the effort to assure survival of the Bill of Rights. Press releases and news clips can be accessed through the A.C.L.U's extensive collection. A file of recent Supreme Court cases related to civil liberties is also maintained. Extensive resources are maintained on each of these issues:

Church and State
Criminal Justice
Cyber Liberties
Death Penalty
Free Speech
HIV/AIDS
Immigrants' Rights
Lesbian and Gay Rights
National Security
Racial Equality
Reproductive Rights
Students' Rights
Voting Rights
Women's Rights
Workplace Rights

[A.C.L.U.]

America Vote, The National Voting Town Hall

Comment

http://www.csn.net/vote/

Participate in this online "Citizens' Referendum on Pending Federal Legislation." Read descriptions of major legislation being considered in the U.S. Congress and participate in (or simply eavesdrop on) online discussions of the issue before casting your vote on each bill. Weekly postings reveal the votes of all participants. A very informative, up-to-date citizenship forum.

Anatomy of a Murder: A Trip Through Our Nation's Legal Justice System

A+

Comment

http://tqd.advanced.org/2760/

A winner in the ThinkQuest '96 student competition, this splendid tutorial guides users through the maze of the legal justice system as they follow a murder suspect from arrest through trial. This well-researched, multimedia lesson will hold the attention of the most reluctant learners. The legal nuances of the criminal prosecution of accused murders are detailed in clear and accurate language. A hypertext glossary helps with the legal terms. What a great learning experience!

[Michael Morley, Chris Stiner, and Michael Hammer; Cranford High School, Cranford, NJ]

Comment	**Are You a Liberal or a Conservative?**
	http://www.c-span.org/book.htm
	Students can complete this 25-item multiple choice quiz to determine whether their basic beliefs align more with the political right or left.
	[C-Span Online]
Comment	**Avalon Project**
	http://www.yale.edu/lawweb/avalon/purpose.htm
	This is a massive collection of important documents from the fields of law, economics, government, history, diplomacy, and politics. The text is linked to related documents. Hypertext annotations and indexes enhance the reader's ability to understand these important records.
	Major collections of documents cluster in the following categories:
	British-American Diplomacy Confederate States of America: Papers Economic and Legal Treatises The Federalist Papers Franco-American Diplomacy The Jefferson Papers Laws of War: Hague Conventions Madison's Notes on Debates in the Federal Convention of 1787 Nazi-Soviet Relations 1939-1941 Nuremberg War Crimes Trial World War II Documents: 1940-1945
	The Avalon Project will no doubt contain controversial documents. Their inclusion does not indicate endorsement of the contents nor sympathy with the ideology, doctrines, or means employed by their authors. They are included for balance and because in some cases they are, by our definition, a supporting document.
	[Yale Law School]
Comment	**Budget of the United States**
	http://www.doc.gov/BudgetFY97/index.html
	Download the official budget of the U.S. government. See "A Citizen's Guide to the Federal Budget" for summary data on

where the money comes from and where it goes. Additional details on the national debt are also provided.

[U.S. Office of Management and Budget]

Comment	**Center for Civic Education** http://www.primenet.com:80/~cce/index.html Why do we need governments? Exploring the answers to this question constitute only one of eleven lessons housed in this site devoted to the promotion of civic education. Several lessons for each grade level are included. Related publications, curriculum materials, and reports are also available. [Center for Civic Education]
Comment	**Citizenship Activities for K-6** http://www.eduplace.com/ss/autoact/ss_3.html A small collection of classroom activities for developing citizenship for elementary grade levels. [Houghton Mifflin Company]
Comment	**Congressional Quarterly Vote Watcher** http://pathfinder.com/@@BP*54wUAaoREqhnd/CQ/ Follow the voting records of senators and representatives. [Congressional Quarterly Magazine]
Comment	**Congressional Quarterly's VoteWatch** http://pathfinder.com/@@k*4C2AYAwJZgPwCD/CQ/ *Congressional Quarterly's* professional staff provides daily, "real time" reports of House and Senate legislative decisions. "Every yea and nay is recorded, tracked and analyzed in painstaking, unbiased detail." Past voting records can be searched in a variety of ways, by particular member or on a specific bill. [Congressional Quarterly Inc.]
Comment	**Congressional Record** http://thomas.loc.gov/j105/major105-1.html

Access the official record of the proceedings of the U.S. Congress. An extensive index of this legislative archive facilitates topical searches.

[United States Congress]

Constitution of the United States

Comment

http://www.access.gpo.gov/congress/senate/constitution/index.html

Since its inception, 27 amendments to the Constitution have been ratified; six were passed on to the states but failed to gain ratification. Discover what they were at this excellent government site. An annotated record of the U.S. Constitution, the Bill of Rights, and other amendments, as well as annotations of cases decided by the Supreme Court, make this a unique and useful site.

[United States Senate, Government Printing Office]

Debt Distortion

Comment

http://www.thirdmil.org/debt/debt.cgi

Students complete a form indicating how they believe the U.S. budget is distributed before checking their estimates with reality. This is a motivating, high-interest activity, whether completed online or used as a paper and pencil lesson.

[Third Millennium, a national, non-partisan, non-profit organization]

Democratic Party

Comment

http://www.democrats.org/

Obviously a partisan view of the U.S. political scene. Combined with a visit to the Republican Web site, many lessons on differentiating fact from opinion could be devised.

[Democratic National Committee]

Federal Bureau of Investigation

Comment

http://www.fbi.gov/

Read the online version of the 387-page book *Crime in the United States* (requires Acrobat Reader), view the F.B.I's "Most Wanted" list, or obtain data on crime statistics.

[Federal Bureau of Investigation]

Comment	**The FedWorld FTP site**
	
	http://www.fedworld.gov/ftp.htm
	
	FedWorld provides FTP access to over 10,000 data files from an array of U.S. government offices. All files can be downloaded to your computer. The master index is updated daily. Convenient keyword searches permit a user to search more than 90 directories for potentially useful items. A short help document gives easy-to-understand directions for conducting a search. A valuable starting point for seeking information related to any governmental function. Examples of available files:
	
	    Federal job announcements
	    White House press releases
	    IRS tax information
	    Cancer information
	
	[U.S. Department of Commerce]

Comment	**Freedom of Information Act** http://www.spj.org/foia/index.htm *Quill* magazine's annual issue devoted to the Freedom of Information Act became this fact-filled Web site. Valuable links are provided to facilitate use of the F.O.I.A. to locate information. [Society of Professional Journalists]

Comment	**Government Lesson Plans**
	
	http://www.primenet.com:80/~cce/lesson-plans.html
	
	Discover a variety of motivating lesson plans for upper elementary, middle, and high school students. The current listing features the following lessons:
	
	    Why Do We Need Authority?
	    What Are the Possible Consequences of Privacy?
	    How Can You Decide among Competing Responsibilities?
	    What Intellectual Tools Are Useful in Making Decisions about Issues of Corrective Justice?
	    What Is a Republican Government?
	    Why Do We Need a Government?
	    How Can Citizens Participate?
	    What Did the Founders Learn about Rights from Studying British History?
	    What Can Be Learned from an International Perspective on Human Rights?
	
	[Center for Civic Education]

Comment	### Government Printing Office http://www.access.gpo.gov/su_docs/aces/aaces001.html The Congressional Record, congressional bills, *The Federal Register,* and other federal government information are available online via GPO Access, a service of the U.S. Government Printing Office. Online searches are easily run with a user-friendly search engine. [United States Government Printing Office]
Comment	### Green Parties http://www.rahul.net/greens/ This political party (or loose affiliation of "Green" parties worldwide) advocates wiser use of the world's natural resources and protection of the environment. Download the "Original Ten Key Values of the Green Committees of Correspondence" and other documents detailing their platform. [Cameron L. Spitzer of the Green Party of Santa Clara County]
Comment	### Gutenberg List of Political Writings http://www.w3.org/pub/DataSources/bySubject/Literature/ Gutenberg/ Politics.html Access the original text of 30 documents influencing the course of democracy in the United States. Among these prominent political writings: The Declaration of Independence of the United States of America The Bill of Rights of the United States of America *The Republic* by Plato The Gettysburg Address of USA President Abraham Lincoln The Constitution of the United States of America "Give Me Liberty or Give Me Death," by Patrick Henry The Mayflower Compact Manifesto of the Communist Party by Friedrich Engels The Federalist Papers *Civil Disobedience* by Henry David Thoreau *Common Sense* by Thomas Paine The Inaugural Address of USA President John F. Kennedy [Project Gutenberg]

Comment	**Historical Congressional Documents** http://lcweb2.loc.gov/const/mdbquery.html Conduct online keyword searches of historical U.S. government documents, including the Declaration of Independence, the Federalist Papers, the Constitution, and early congressional documents. [Library of Congress]
Comment	**In Congress Assembled: Continuity and Change in the Governing of the United States** http://lcweb2.loc.gov/ammem/ndlpedu/lessons/constitu/conintro.html Another outstanding resource from the nation's library, four lesson plans use primary resources to examine "continuity and change in the governing of the United States." In one lesson, students grapple with the same issues confronted by the first Congress. Another invites elementary school students to consider the issue of declaring national holidays. High school students use primary source documents online from the Library of Congress to debate the issues involved in the writing of the Constitution and Bill of Rights. [Library of Congress]
Comment	**Infomine: Government Information** http://lib-www.ucr.edu/govinfo.html What a reference tool! This mega-site organizes a massive amount of information from numerous data sources in an easy-to-use, one-stop virtual library—a collection of collections. Definitely bookmark this page. It will become a favorite. [Library of the University of California, Riverside]
Comment	**Internet Law Library** http://www.pls.com:8001/ A great starting point for anything related to the law. This directory provides easy access to over 1,600 law-related resources on the Internet. Major topics: U.S. federal laws U.S. state and territorial laws

A+

> Laws of other nations
> Treaties and international law
> Laws of all jurisdictions (arranged by subject)
> Law school library catalogues and services
> Attorney and legal profession directories
> Reviews of law books

[The U.S. House of Representatives]

Comment

The Jefferson Project

http://www.voxpop.org/jefferson/

This superb collection of Web sites related to democracy and federal, state, and local government in the United States links dozens of resources assembled in categories, such as: Personalities, Parties, Political News, Political Humor, The Left, The Right, and Political Watchdogs. A great all-round starting point for all things political.

[Stardot Consulting, Ltd.]

A+

Comment

Juristic Park

http://www.public.usit.net/mtmartin/jurpark.htm

Someone was bound to pick this name for a Web page covering the judicial system. More than a catchy name, splendid reference resources can be found here.

[Juristic Cites]

Comment

Ladies of the House...and Senate

http://members.tripod.com/~tonyap/women.html

This unique resource includes Web pages for all the female members of Congress. Biographical information and photos are included.

[Tonya Pettigrew]

Comment

Law Center

http://205.181.114.35/

The latest information, comment, and discussion of major trials, Supreme Court rulings, or events affecting the judicial branch of government can be found in this pleasantly designed Web site. Feature articles are often written by some of the best law professors and practicing attorneys in the country. Check out the "Courtroom Challenge," where a real Supreme Court landmark case is presented. After researching facts, the law, and other factors, the user issues a ruling, which is then verified against the high court's final decision. Though the content is excellent for background research, be sure to read the copyright restrictions on copying any materials from this site. Remember the focus of this site on justice and criminal prosecution!

[Court TV Network, American Lawyer Media]

Comment

Law Journal Extra

http://www.ljx.com/

Though intended primarily for lawyers, this site is filled with information about a wide range of legal issues, court rulings, law practice, and electronic links to over fifty law libraries, archives, and Internet mailing lists. The "News Updates" summaries should prove invaluable in planning lessons on current legal issues, such as censorship of the Internet.

[The New York Law Publishing Company]

A+

Comment

Lawmarks

http://www.cclabs.missouri.edu/~tbrown/lawmarks/

In this well-organized online law library dozens of links to legal resources can be found under such categories as Rules of Court, Legal Directories, Federal Documents, Civil Liberties, and American Politics.

[North American Communications Corporation, University of Missouri-Columbia, and Entropy, Inc.]

Comment

Legal Information Institute

http://www.law.cornell.edu/statutes.html

What are the uniform rules of evidence? Who has the power to impeach the Texas Governor? Find out at this splendid Web site. The federal Constitution and the U.S. Code (of all laws enacted by Congress), as well as most state constitutions and statutes, are accessible through this site.

[Cornell Law School]

Comment	LEGI-SLATE http://www.legislate.com/index.htm Get a plain-English, inside view of how the government works. Timely reports from this online service provide daily updates on congressional and regulatory actions. Each weekday, "News of the Day" provides an articulate analysis of at least one major legislative issue. [*The Washington Post*]

Comment	**Lesson Plans for Law**
	
	http://www.digicity.com/lesson/l_law.htm
	
	An excellent set of 27 lesson plans and student activities is accessible through this curriculum jumplist. Most are for high-school-level students, though a few are targeted for middle school students. A small sampling of lessons:
	
	    Arrest
	    Due Process: Search and Seizure
	    How a Bill Becomes a Law
	    Introduction of Restrictions on Freedom of Speech
	    Justice, Is It Fair?
	    Laws: Who Needs Them?
	    The Night Thoreau Spent in Jail
	    Shoplifting Simulation
	
	[The Education Station]

Comment	**Libertarian Web** http://www.libertarian.org/ The Libertarians usually appear on the presidential ballot, but few people know their platform. Check out their Web page for a view of national and world events different from what you'll get from the Republican or Democratic parties. [Libertarian Party]
Comment	**Mother Jones 400** http://www.mojones.com/coinop_congress/mojo_400/mojo_400.html Who are the biggest contributors to political campaigns? *Mother Jones*, the watchdog journal, tells names and

amounts in their list of the "elite Fat Cats." Efforts toward campaign reform initiatives are frequently discussed.

[Foundation for National Progress]

National Election Studies

Comment

http://www.umich.edu:80/~nes/resourcs/nesguide/gd-index.htm

The N.E.S. Guide to Public Opinion and Electoral Behavior provides instant access to tables and graphs of public opinion and election results since 1952. The data displays are organized into eight topics:

    Social and Religious Characteristics of the Electorate
    Partisanship and Evaluation of the Political Parties
    Ideological Self-Identification
    Public Opinion on Public Policy Issues
    Support for the Political System
    Political Involvement and Participation in Politics
    Evaluation of the Presidential Candidates
    Evaluation of Congressional Candidates

[U.S. National Science Foundation funded; Center for Political Studies at The University of Michigan's Institute for Social Research]

The New Republic

Comment

http://www.enews.com/magazines/tnr/

The online version of the prestigious journal of political opinion, featuring insightful, colorful political commentary by award-winning writers.

[*The New Republic* via The Electronic Newsstand]

Parliamentary Internet Newsletter

Comment

http://parli.com/news1112.htm

The "Parliamentary Internet Newsletter" is devoted to teaching the basics of running formal meetings. This is a valuable resource, offering many helpful suggestions.

[Robert McConnell Productions]

Parliamentary Procedure: A Very Short Course

Comment

http://www.fairnet.org/VCD/PProc/default.html

An excellent introduction to the principles of "Robert's Rules of Procedure," an American adaptation of "Robert's Rules of Order." The simple language and clear organization of the tutorial make this a very useful resource.

[James D. DeWitt, Volunteer Action Center of the United Way of the Tanana Valle]

Police Officer's Internet Directory

Comment

http://www.officer.com/

Its claim that "Everything on the Web that's law enforcement-related can be found here, arranged in an orderly, easy-to-navigate fashion" appears to be substantiated. Though wholly link-reliant, the mass of information included makes this a site worth a visit. The section on "Hate Groups, Terrorists, & Radicals" is enlightening. There are links to several hate group Web pages (e.g., Aryan Nations, Skin-Net White Power Listings, The Watchman, The Zündelsite). Some of these groups are blatantly racist and anti-Semitic, so be very cautious of how you might use their content. A visit to the hate groups' Web pages does certainly give a glimpse of the intensity of their positions. An interesting thought to ponder: some of your students may have relatives involved with one of these groups.

[James Meredith]

Project Vote Smart

Comment

http://www.vote-smart.org/

This organization is devoted to "providing citizens/voters with information about the political system, issues, candidates and elected officials." Download the *U.S. Government: Owner's Manual* filled with information on every U.S. Senator and Representative including their biographies, campaign contributors, performance evaluations, and voting records. Other items available at this Web site:

> Photos and audio text of speeches by the President, members of Congress and the Cabinet
> Supreme Court decisions and biographies of the Justices
> Backgrounds of governors and state legislators, and the text of state laws
> Issue briefs from national, regional, and local interest groups
> Historical documents and materials from research libraries and archives

[The Center for National Independence in Politics, a national nonpartisan organization]

Comment	**Republican National Committee** http://rnc.org/hq/ Check out the G.O.P's home page for the official party plat-form and other information about Republican views and candidates. For contrast, assign students to compare the same issues on the Democrat's Web page. [Republican National Committee]
Comment	**Right Side of the Web** http://www.clark.net:80/pub/jeffd/index.html This Web side presenting the conservative political view-point includes links to Rush Limbaugh and other right-wing political commentators. [Conservative Internet Connections Group]
Comment	**Rock the Vote** http://www.rockthevote.org/ Dedicated to educating young people on the important issues of the day and motivating them to vote, this colorful, graph-ics-filled Web site provides a huge archive of information on contemporary social and political issues, such as violence, censorship, and race relations. [Rock the Vote Foundation]
Comment	**Roll Call Online** http://www.rollcall.com/ Since 1955 this private journalistic enterprise has reported on Congress with a somewhat different slant, highlighting the three Ps: people, politics, and process. Now an electronic edition provides the hottest news on Congressional activities and personalities. [Roll Call, Inc.]
Comment	**Social Security Teachers Kit** http://www.ssa.gov/teacher/teacher.html Download five lesson plans which explain the social security system to high school students. Helpful fact sheets, student

handouts, and quizzes are included. A free 25-minute video-tape can be obtained by sending a blank 60-minute VHS tape.

[Social Security Administration]

Supreme Court Cases

Comment

http://supct.law.cornell.edu/supct/

Through this site teachers and students can access all opinions of the court issued since May of 1990 and 300 of the most important historical Supreme Court decisions before that date. An alphabetic index of keywords provides links to relevant cases and usually information in three forms: syllabus, full decision, or edited decision. This is the best place to start if you are looking for a Supreme Court decision on a specific topic. The glossary of legal terms could prove very valuable.

[Cornell University Law School]

THOMAS: Legislative Information on the Internet

Comment

http://thomas.loc.gov/

Access copies of current legislation as well as the addresses, phone numbers, and e-mail addresses of members of Congress. Download summaries of bills and follow them through the political process. Fortunately, their powerful search engine facilitates navigating this mass of data.

[United States Congress]

Turn Left

Comment

http://www.cjnetworks.com/~cubsfan/liberal.html

Espousing a distinctly liberal viewpoint, *Turn Left* explains what liberals believe and lists their self-proclaimed accomplishments.

[Mike Silverman]

U.S. Capitol

Comment

http://www.aoc.gov/

The official home page of the nation's Capitol Building, seat of the United States Congress, includes an account of the

Capitol's construction history, its architectural features and historic spaces, the Capitol Grounds, treasured works of art at the Capitol, the U.S. Botanical Garden, and current and recent projects at the Capitol.

[Architect of the Capitol, Office of the Curator]

U.S. Code

Comment

http://law.house.gov:80/usc.htm

Conduct a topic search of the U.S. Code, accessing all laws ever passed by the United States Congress.

[United States House of Representatives]

U.S. Government Internet Resources

Comment

http://ds.internic.net/ds/gov.html

A virtual gateway to almost everything the federal government has on the Internet. Use the efficient search engines for keyword searches or browse the well-organized index arranged by governmental branch. The "Blue Pages" directory provides phone numbers, addresses, and e-mail addresses of thousands of federal, state, local, and Canadian governmental officials. City information, weather, and yellow pages of businesses are accessible bonus sections.

[National Science Foundation, AT&T and Network Solutions, Inc.]

U.S. Historical Documents

Comment

http://www.law.uoknor.edu/ushist.html

From the Mayflower Compact to President Clinton's second inaugural address, this electronic archive houses major historical documents related to the evolution of the United States government. This Web site serves as a good link to dozens of digitized versions of original historical documents.

[The University of Oklahoma Law Center]

U.S. House of Representatives

Comment

http://www.house.gov/

Access legislative information about members and committees of the House of Representatives at their official Web site. Major topic areas included in this inviting resource:

The Legislative Process
Schedules for the Legislative Activity of the House of
Representatives.
Who's Who and How To Contact Them
Leadership
Organization and Operations
Laws
Educational Resources
Empowering the Citizen

[U.S. House of Representatives]

U.S. Senate

Comment

http://www.senate.gov/

The official home page of the United States Senate provides basic information about the Senators and their leadership, recent committee and legislative activities, a Frequently Asked Questions file, e-mail addresses, and links to other government sites. Special features of the site:

The Senate Historical Office
Senate Art and Historical Collections
Brief History of the Senate
Publications about the United States Senate
Planning Your Visit to the Senate
A Virtual Tour of the U.S. Capitol
The Legislative Process
A Glossary of Senate Terms

[United States Senate]

Vote Smart

Comment

http://www.vote-smart.org/about/

Project Vote Smart, sponsored by a national nonpartisan organization, seeks to provide citizens with information about the political issues, candidates, and elected officials. Though the Web page is especially full of information during election campaigns, it does provide worthwhile year-round services. During off-election years the emphasis is upon monitoring elected officials. Extensive data are presented on campaign finances, performance evaluations, voting records, and key legislation.

[The Center for National Independence in Politics]

Comment	### What Is? http://www.tncrimlaw.com/what_is/index.html In plain language this very informative Web site explains "what happens when a person is charged with an alleged crime." All adolescents should rummage through this candid and factual Web site. A sampling of the questions answered: What are my rights? What is bond or bail? What is an arraignment? What is a preliminary hearing? What is a grand jury? What is circuit or criminal court? What is a trial basically like? What is an appeal? [TnCrimLaw]
Comment	### White House http://www.whitehouse.gov/WH/Welcome.html The official Web site for the President of the United States and the White House highlights the executive branch, the executive mansion/office, and its occupants. A massive amount of information about the federal government can be accessed through this home page. Use the "Virtual Library" to search White House documents, view photographs, and hear speeches. The site is structured around major sections: The President & Vice President Direct Access to Federal Services Interactive Citizens' Handbook What's New What's Happening at the White House—The Toughest Job In the World White House for Kids White House History and Tours Past Presidents and First Families The Briefing Room [The White House]
Comment	### Your Money Matters http://www.ustreas.gov/treasury/whatsnew/newcur/ This official U.S. Treasury Web site describes the security changes in the redesigned U.S. currency. Detailed descrip-

tions of measures, such as color-shifting Ink and microprinting, are depicted with colorful graphics, including images of the new bills.

[United States Department of Treasury]

ELECTRONIC MAILING LISTS: GOVERNMENT

Many electronic mailing lists focus on topics of interest to government teachers and students. It is easy to subscribe. For example, to subscribe to the mailing list AFAS-L on African American studies:

Send an e-mail message to: LISTSERV@KENTVM.KEN.EDU

Usually it is best to leave the "Subject" line blank. If your e-mail software requires something in the subject line, simply type a period.

Enter the message: subscribe AFAS-L <your name>

Remember to enter your name instead of John Doe.

The format for the message is: subscribe <List_Name> <Your_Full_Name>

Afas-L
African American studies
E-mail to: LISTSERV@KENTVM.KEN.EDU

America
Forum focusing on U.S. government and foreign trade
E-mail to: MAILSERV@XAMIGA.LINET.ORG

Apgovpol
Forum for Advanced Placement American government teachers
E-mail to: LISTSERV@ASUVM.INRE.ASU.EDU

Arms-L
Arms proliferation discussion
E-mail to: LISTSERV@BUACCA.BU.EDU

Cd4Urban
Development of urban communities
E-mail to: LISTPROC@U.WASHINGTON.EDU

Civic-Values
Discussion of community and neighborhood values
E-mail to: LISTPROC@CIVIC.NET

Cjust-L
Criminal justice issues
E-mail to: LISTSERV@CUNYVM.CUNY.EDU

Complaw-L
Comparative law forum
E-mail to: LISTSERV@USC.EDU

Cong-Reform
Congressional reform forum sponsored by Ralph Nader
E-mail to: ESSENTIAL.ORG

Congress-L
U.S. Congress forum sponsored by the Carl Albert Center
E-mail to: LISTSERV@UOKNOR.EDU

Dem-Digitals
Democratic party enthusiasts meet here
E-mail to: LISTSERV@NETCOM.COM

Dem-Net
US Democratic party forum
E-mail to: LISTSERV@NETCOM.COM

Dem-Net-Digest
More Democratic party discussion
E-mail to: DEM-NET-DIGEST-REQUEST@WEBCOM.COM

Dispute-Res
Teaching conflict resolution
E-mail to: LISTSERV@LISTSERV.LAW.CORNELL.EDU

Ecol-Econ
Ecological economics forum
E-mail to: LISTSERV@CSF.COLORADO.EDU

Edlaw
Educational law
E-mail to: LISTSERV@UKCC.UKY.EDU

Elections-Reform
Election reform discussion
E-mail to: MAJORDOMO@IGC.APC.ORG

Geopol
Political geography
E-mail to: LISTSERV@UKCC.UKY.EDU

Govmanag

Discussion of management in government

E-mail to: LISTSERV@LIST.NIH.GOV

Humanrights-L

Human rights and laws around the world

E-mail to: LISTSERV@ACC.WUACC.EDU

Humanrights-L

Human rights forum

E-mail to: LISTSERV@LAWLIB.WUACC.EDU

Lawsoc-L

Canadian law and society

E-mail to: LAWSOC-L-REQUEST@CC.UMANITOBA.CA

Lawsrc-L

Legal resources on the Internet

E-mail to: LISTSERV@LISTSERV.LAW.CORNELL.EDU

Liibulletin

Immediate posting of U.S. Supreme Court decisions

E-mail to: LISTSERV@LISTSERV.LAW.CORNELL.EDU

Marxism

Discussion of the theories of Marx and Engels

E-mail to: MAJORDOMO@WORLD.STD.COM

Marxism General

More on Marx and Engels

E-mail to: MAJORDOMO@LISTS.VILLAGE.VIRGINIA.EDU

Povertylaw-L

Legal issues related to poverty

E-mail to: LISTSERV@LAWLIB.WUACC.EDU

Prelaw-Students-L

Discussion list for prelaw students

E-mail to: LISTSERV@LAWLIB.WUACC.EDU

Privacy

Privacy, especially in Cyberspace

E-mail to: LISTSERV@VORTEX.COM

Statepol

State politics

E-mail to: LISTSERV@WVNVM.WVNET.EDU

UNCJIN-L
United Nations Criminal Justice Information Network
E-mail to: LISTSERV@ALBNYVM1.EDU

Newsgroups: Government

alt.foia	Freedom of Information Act
alt.politics.bush	Politics in the George Bush administration
alt.politics.clinton	Politics during the Clinton administration
alt.politics.datahighway	Legal aspects of the Internet
alt.politics.democrats.d	Discussion of Democratic party
alt.politics.economics	Discussion of U.S. economic policies
alt.politics.elections	Politics and U.S. elections
alt.politics.equality	Issues surrounding the politics of equality
alt.politics.greens	The ecology and related political issues
alt.politics.immigration	Discussion of the immigration politics
alt.politics.libertarian	Libertarian's newsgroup
alt.politics.media	Politics and the public media
alt.politics.org.cia	Issues related to the CIA
alt.politics.org.fbi	Politics of the Federal Bureau of Investigation
alt.politics.org.misc	General discussion of political organizations
alt.politics.org.nsa	National Security Agency actions and issues
alt.politics.org.un	General discussion of United Nations politics
alt.politics.radical-left	Radical Leftist politics
alt.politics.reform	Reform of political process
alt.politics.usa	Politics in the U.S.
alt.politics.usa.congress	Political arena of the U.S. Congress
alt.politics.usa.constitution	Politics and the U.S. Constitution
alt.politics.usa.misc	General discussion of U.S. politics

Newsgroups: Government (Continued)

alt.politics.usa.republican	Republican party politics
alt.society.civil-disob	Discussion of civil disobediance
misc.immigration.usa	Issues related to immigration to the U.S.
opinions.supreme.court	Moderated discussion of Supreme Court Opinions
soc.politics	Political systems & problems (moderated)
soc.politics.arms-d	Issues of arms proliferation through the world
talk.politics.drugs	Mostly the U.S. war on drugs
talk.politics.guns	Gun control, the NRA, and the Second Amendment
talk.politics.libertarian	Libertarian view of political issues
talk.politics.medicine	Political aspects of medicine in America
talk.politics.space	Politics of America's space program
talk.politics.theory	Discussion of political theories and systems

CURRENT EVENTS

Best Web Sites: Current Events

Comment	**Africa News Online: Gateway to the Continent** http://www.africanews.org/ Extensive coverage of events throughout Africa is updated daily at this colorful Web site. Students checking this news source may find a vantage point different from that offered by American news organizations. Special sections on "Africa and the U.S." and "Africa and the U.N." highlight international political events from the African vantage point. [African News Service]
Comment	**AllPolitics** http://cgi.pathfinder.com/@@smNFJQcA4aX@a9n2/ cgi-bin/boards/read/11 Enthusiatistic, yet generally civil discussion of wide-ranging political issues. Flaming is actively discouraged by the sponsors. [*Time* Magazine and CNN]
Comment	**American Newspeak** http://www.scn.org/news/newspeak/ George Orwell coined the term "newspeak" to describe meaningless doublethink, an art continuing to be perfected by political and special interest spokepersons seeking to influence American public opinion. Political satirist Wayne Grytting highlights the best examples of newspeak from each week's news items. Most would be hilarious if they weren't actually intended to be taken seriously. Some great discussion starters here. [Wayne Grytting]
Comment	**American Prospect** http://epn.org/prospect.html#who Electronic edition of the liberal magazine which "seeks to provide a forum for working through the heated controversies and hard choices." Develop valuable critical thinking lessons by having students compare items from this publication with those of conservative publications. [New Prospect, Inc.]

Comment	**Amnesty International** http://www.io.org/~amnesty/ This watchdog organization monitors human rights violations around the world. "Searching for the Truth" describes the research process used by Amnesty International to identify these violations. [Amnesty International]
Comment	**Asian Studies WWW Virtual Library** http://coombs.anu.edu.au/WWWVL-AsianStudies.html Magnificent starting point for researching any aspect of Asia. Updated daily, this massive collection tracks new developments in each of the Asian countries. Be sure to check the "What's New in Asian Studies" online newsletter. Meticulous care has been taken to include only links of the highest quality. [Australian National University]
Comment	**Atlantic Unbound** http://www.TheAtlantic.com/ The electronic edition of *Atlantic Monthly* magazine provides thoughtful analyses of the major issues of the day by some of the world's top writers and thinkers. Check out "Flashbacks," thematic collections of previous articles from the *Atlantic's* archives, for well-researched, in-depth essays. A small sampling of these outstanding articles: Affirmative Action, Copyright Piracy, Death Penalty, Euthanasia, Flat-Tax, Tobacco Industry, and Welfare. Bookmark this site and check back often. [The Atlantic Monthly]
Comment	**BBC** http://www.bbc.co.uk/index/search.html Use this link to conduct keyword searches of the British Broadcasting Corporation's program archives for an alternative perspective on world news. [British Broadcasting Corporation]

Comment	**Boston Globe—Discussions** http://www.boston.com/cgi-bin/ The esteemed newspaper sponsors 14 discussion areas, including: National/Foreign, Metro/Region, Opinion, Business. [Boston Globe]
Comment	**C-SPAN Online** http://www.c-span.org/ Sponsored by the public affairs cable television channel, C-SPAN Online promotes and augments its on-air broadcasts. Many teachers utilize live or recorded C-SPAN national and world events programming in their classrooms. Regular programming includes gavel-to-gavel coverage of the U.S. House of Representatives and Senate (on C-SPAN2), Congressional hearings, White House press conferences, and other educational programming. Teachers are granted liberal permission to copy and use the commercial-free C-Span programs for educational purposes. The "C-SPAN Lesson Plans" section offers instructional ideas to accompany its broadcasts. The "C-SPAN in the Classroom Bulletin Board" invites teachers to exchange ideas on teaching current events topics, an excellent resource. [National Cable Satellite Corp.]
Comment	**Cafe Utne (free registration required)** http://www.utne.com/motet/bin/home Discussions are invited in 45 individual conference areas, such as current events, politics, education, gender issues, world affairs, society, and work/money. [*Utne Reader*]
Comment	**Central Europe Online** http://www.centraleurope.com/ Superb, in-depth coverage of events in the Central European nations. Colorful graphics and crisp writing make this a must-see resource for news of this region. [European Information Network]

A+

Central Intelligence Agency Publications

Comment

http://www.odci.gov/cia/publications/pubs.html

Many will be pleasantly surprised at the high-quality, well-researched publications freely available via the CIA home page. Online keyword searches of all CIA publications are possible. A partial listing of available documents:

> The World Factbook
> Factbook on Intelligence
> Chiefs of State and Cabinet Members of Foreign Governments
> Handbook of International Economic Statistics
> Intelligence in the War of Independence
> CIA Maps and Publications Released to the Public
> The Balkans Regional Atlas

[Central Intelligence Agency]

A+

Children's Express News Service

Comment

http://www.ce.org/

This electronic newspaper is produced by young folks, ages 8-18. Their splendid Web site highlights current events having the greatest potential impact upon the lives of the world's youth. The award-winning site also contains an interactive page permitting students around the world to comment on current news items.

[Children's Express Foundation, Inc.]

Common Cause

Comment

http.//www.commoncause.org/

This grassroots lobbying group advertises itself as a "nonprofit, nonpartisan citizens' lobbying organization promoting open, honest and accountable government." It sponsors extensive research efforts in public policy issues, such as campaign financing. The group often asks the difficult (and sometimes embarrassing) questions in seeking to keep our political leaders accountable. Extensive data including articles and press releases are available through its Web site.

[Common Cause]

Comment	### Contemporary Conflicts in Africa http://www.synapse.net/~acdi20/welcome.htm Devoted exclusively to covering the "hot spots" on the African continent, special coverage focuses upon peacekeeping efforts and conflict management. Maps of the individual countries are available through this link. [Yves Contamine]
Comment	### Cuba Internet Resources http://ix.urz.uni-heidelberg.de/~pklee/Cuba/ Connect to dozens of Internet resources on Cuba in this exhibit constructed of materials from the Soviet Archive. Content ranges from the Cuban Missile Crisis to samples of Cuban music. Links to Mailing list CUBA-L (Spanish or English) and the USENET Newsgroup soc.culture.cuba are also available through this Web site. [Peter Klee, University of Heidelberg]
Comment	### Disinformation http://www.disinfo.com/ Billed as "the subculture search engine," this unusual and interesting resource is devoted to seeking truth, correcting misinformation, and providing alternative viewpoints to those presented in mainstream news media. Through links to a variety of online news sources, thought-provoking viewpoints cover propaganda, revolutionaries, censorship, counterculture, and counterintelligence. [Razorfish Subnetwork]
Comments	### Doonesbury Electronic Townhall—Soundbytes http://www.doonesbury.com/ The official homepage of cartoonist Gary Trudeau's Doonesbury offers a thought-provoking, if not somewhat cynical, view of current political events and contemporary American society. Readers are invited to join in the lively discussion through the "Soundbytes" forum. Weekday updates on the site provide plenty of mental fodder. [Mindscape, Inc. and G. B. Trudeau]

Comment	**Electronic Newsstand** http://www.enews.com/ The Electronic Newsstand lives up to its billing as the "monster magazine list," providing well-organized hypertext links to over 2,000 online magazines. [Enews]
Comment	**Embassy Page** http://www.embpage.org/ Links to all embassies and consulates having Web pages are listed in this clearinghouse. [GlobeScope Internet Services]
Comment	**EUROLINK: The Pan European Web Index** http://www.syselog.com/eurolink/ Data extracted from national databases provide extensive background information on fifteen European countries. [Syselog Co.]
Comment	**Europa** http://europa.eu.int/ The European Union, started in the 1950s with six member countries, has grown to fifteen states. A 1993 treaty paves the way for economic and monetary union and a single currency. Its official Web site provides current information on the history, policies, and current news of this unique multinational effort. [European Union]
Comment	**Forum One** http://www.ForumOne.com/ Search over 59,000 discussion forums to find the one which fits your interests. [Forum One Communications Corporation]

Comment	**Friends and Partners** http://www.friends-partners.org/friends/home. htmlopt-tables-mac-e nglish- Developed jointly by American and Russian citizens to improve mutual understanding, Friends and Partners provides an opportunity to exchange information on both countries' histories, art, literature, music, religion, languages, and educational and scientific resources. The "Community Corner" includes a coffee house where participants from around the world can exchange messages on an interactive bulletin board. An interactive real-time "Community Chat" section permits immediate interaction with persons from Russia and other countries. An e-mail listserv discussion list is also available to browse or join. [U.S. State Department, NATO, Sun Microsystems, the International Science Foundation, Esper Systems, RELARN, Stack, Inc., Pushchino Institute of Biochemistry and Physiology of Microorganisms, and The University of Tennessee]
Comment	**Gerben News** http://www.cs.vu.nl/~gerben/news.html Check out world events in online editions of *The Cambodia Times*, *The Vancouver Echo*, *Albanian Times*, *The Jerusalem Post*, or dozens of other newspapers from around the world. An extensive listing of U.S. newspapers is also provided. Some of the third-world newspapers are not updated very regularly, though most are less than two days old. This site is arguably the most extensive listing of electronic world news sources on the Net. [Gerben Vos]
Comment	**HateWatch** http://hatewatch.org/noframe.html The Internet has provided an unprecedented world-wide soapbox for so-called hate groups who advocate violence against or hostility toward ethnic or cultural groups. HateWatch monitors the Internet activities of these hate groups and seeks to inform the public of the threat they pose. [HateWatch, Inc.]

Comment	**Hot Topics in RAND Research** http://www.rand.org/hot/ A non-profit institution, RAND (an acronym for Research and Development) seeks to enhance public policy through high-quality, objective research and analyses. Access the thinking of this think tank's best minds through concise reports on a spectrum of issues. Recent "Hot Topics" include: How Immigrants Fare in U.S. Education Diverting Children from a Life of Crime: What Are the Costs and Benefits? Guarding against Ground Attacks on U.S. Air Force Bases An Air Force for Crises and Lesser Conflicts Choosing an Alternative to Tort When Do They Settle Down? Young People in the U.S. Labor Market Student Performance and the Changing American Family The Decline of the U.S. Machine-Tool Industry and Prospects for Recovery China: Domestic Change and Foreign Policy [RAND]
Comment	**Idea Central** http://epn.org/idea/ This award-winning virtual magazine presents insightful news analyses which exceed the sound bites offered by many news sources. Content includes the following areas: Economics and Politics Welfare and Families Education Civic Participation Health Policy Media Old & New [Electronic Policy Network]
Comment	**Kids Web Japan** http://www.jinjapan.org/kidsweb/index.html Designed for students age 10-14 years, this colorful resource provides a view of Japanese culture, news, politics, and geography. Students will enjoy comparing the account of Japanese school life with their own. The age-appropriate

text, whimsical graphics, and beautiful photographs will hold the attention of almost every student.

[Japan Information Network]

Comment	**LatinoLink** http://www.latinolink.com/ News, chat, and commentary on social and political issues affecting Latinos are featured in this source, providing an alternative perspective on affirmative action, immigration policy, bi-lingual education, and Latino culture. [LatinoLink Enterprises, Inc.]
Comment	**Lincoln-Douglas Debate Complex** http://ourworld.compuserve.com/homepages/Under_World/ Don't be misled by the title of this Web page; it is concerned with more than just the legendary Lincoln-Douglas debates. This is a great resource for information on developing debating skills in high school students.
Comment	**Maps in the News** http://www-map.lib.umn.edu/news.html Each day, this news source features several maps pertaining to the major news events. [John R. Borchert Map Library, University of Minnesota]
Comment	**NBC Worldwide** http://www.nbc.com/worldwide.html NBC's "Asia, Inc." link provides wide-ranging, weekly news items on the many facets of Asia. [National Broadcasting Company]
Comment	**The Nation** http://www.thenation.com/ The digital edition of America's oldest weekly magazine presents an in-depth look at some of the top news stories. The publication claims a "tradition of providing intelligent, accu-

rate and honest reporting and analysis, and countering dis-information, prejudice and shallow thought." Not all stories from the paper version are accessible online. Search the archive of past issues.

[The Nation]

Netizen (free registration required)

Comment

http://www.netizen.com/netizen/threads/

Participate in a digital town hall, featuring discussions on social, political, and journalistic effects of the Internet and other new technologies.

[HotWired Network]

New York Times—Discussion Forums

Comment

http://www.nytimes.com/

Join discussions of national and international current events and politics. Free registration required.

[New York Times]

Number 10 Downing Street

Comment

http://www.number-10.gov.uk/

The official Web site of the British Prime Minister, this site "opens a new door to what the British Government does, news from No. 10 and other Government Web sites." In addition to a virtual tour of the official residence of the B.P.M., biographies of the Prime Minister and the Cabinet Ministers are featured. Transcripts of major speeches and interviews by the Queen, Prime Minister, and other British dignitaries can be downloaded.

[The British Crown]

Online NewsHour

Comment

http://www1.pbs.org/newshour/home.html

View transcripts of the weekday broadcasts of PBS's "NewsHour with Jim Lehrer," featuring background briefings, forums, and an archive of past programs. Some selections are available in RealAudio.

[MacNeil/Lehrer Productions and PBS]

Comment	### Outbreak http://www.outbreak.org/cgi-unreg/dynaserve.exe/index.html Is the next Bubonic Plague just around the corner? This online service provides lay persons as well as medical professionals with up-to-date, accurate information on emerging diseases, such as Eubola or Hemmorhagic Fever. An extensive database (currently over 100 pages) can be navigated easily with a well-constructed Table of Contents. [Pragmatica, Inc.]
Comment	### Peace Corps http://www.peacecorps.gov/ The Peace Corps' World Wise Schools program arranges for over 6,000 former Peace Corps volunteers to visit local classrooms to describe their experiences. These visits can enrich cultural understanding and geography awareness. Classes can exchange correspondence with active Peace Corps volunteers around the world. Outstanding videotapes and study guides featuring Peace Corps countries are available free to teachers. Online information on various countries is also available. [U.S. Peace Corps]
Comment	### Reuters http://www.reuters.com/ The world-wide news reporting service provides up-to-the-minute financial news headlines, some with optional audio and video clips. These multimedia newscasts do require the appropriate plug-ins for your Web browser. [Reuters Limited]
Comment	### Russia Today http://www.russiatoday.com/ This electronic journal provides in-depth news of Russian politics, culture, and economics. Few American publications can provide such complete coverage of Russian news. [European Information Network]

Comment	**Teaching (and Learning) About Japan** http://www.csuohio.edu/history/japan.html A colorful, well-documented online resource providing an in-depth view of contemporary and traditional aspects of life in Japan today. Through original content and selected links to other sites, Dr. Makela provides a great starting point for any teacher looking for useful material on this country. [Lee A. Makela, Department of History, Cleveland State University]
Comment	**TIME.com** http://pathfinder.com/@@i@FpZQUAi4dBIHmS/time/ The online version of *Time*, the news magazine, enhanced with audio and video clips, though the text and graphs version is quite sufficient. "Time Daily" presents weekday updates on major news items. Colorful photographs illustrate most stories and a search engine retrieves items from past issues. Advertising teasers are prominently displayed on the page masthead. [Time Warner]
Comment	**Time—Message Boards** http://pathfinder.com/@@fubWAAYAQ@Ni5rre/boards A wide array of discussion pondering domestic and international topics: Washington, Society, Science & Technology, The Sexes, Health & Medicine, Europe, Asia/Pacific, The Americas, Middle East/Africa, Digital Issues (Cyberspace stuff), and Crime. [Pathfinder.com]
Comment	**Tokyo Kaleidoscoop** http://www.smn.co.jp/ Visit this superb, award-winning online journal for the latest news from a Japanese perspective. The "Hot Asia!" section features news from each of the Asian countries for in-depth coverage of items seldom found in U.S. news sources. Download articles to have students compare with U.S. reports of the same event. English and Japanese language editions are available. [Shima Media Network Inc.]

Comment	**Top 10 News from Asia** http://www.asianmall.com/top10news/ This award-winning news site offers "a vast amount of reliable information about political, business and social issues in Asia from the Asian perspective." Much greater in-depth coverage of Asian events is included than would generally be found in American news sources. [Creative Online Enterprises]
Comment	**Turn Left Interactive** http://www.cjnetworks.com/~cubsfan/interactive.html An interactive haven for liberal folks. Discussions cover a multitude of political, economic, and social issues. [Mike Silverman]
Comment	**U.S. Department of State** http://dosfan.lib.uic.edu/dosfan.html Updates on current policies, peace negotiations, and international "hot spots" are included in the State Department's home page. A well-done page on career opportunities in international diplomacy will interest some students. [United States Department of State]
Comment	**U.S. News Online** http://www.usnews.com/usnews/main.htm Visit the online edition of the weekly news magazine for information on a wide assortment of contemporary topics. Keyword searches of the archive are available. [*U.S. News & World Report*]
Comment	**USA Today** http://www.usatoday.com/ Arguably the most complete daily news source on the Web, featuring concise writing and excellent photography. The online edition of the weekday national newspaper maintains the same high-quality standards as its paper edition. In addition to the "News," section teachers will occasionally find useful lesson content in the "Life" and "What's Hot" sec-

A+

tions. Beyond merely reporting the major events of the day, this sprawling complex of useful content provides a one-stop, up-to-date, virtual library.

[Gannett Co. Inc.]

Ultimate Collection of News Links

Comment

http://pppp.net/links/news/

Heaven for the news junkie, this megasite features over 5,300 links to newspapers, magazines, and news services in virtually every country of the world. The links are organized by continent and country.

[PPPP.net]

United Nations Online

Comment

http://www.serve.com/GEMUN/index.html

This first-rate online simulation encourages students to practice the skills used in the United Nations. Student teams representing assigned countries study issues, write position papers, present resolutions, debate, and seek agreements. Inexpensive student handbooks provide additional support. An excellent skill-building activity.

[United Nations]

United Nations Development Program

Comment

http://www.undp.org/undp/poverty/

It is estimated that 25 million people a year join the ranks of abject poverty. Successful programs to eradicate poverty, as well as personal stories of individuals who have escaped, are described in this U.N. Web site.

[United Nations]

Universal Black Pages

Comment

http://www.ubp.com/

Ambitious Georgia Tech students have striven to make this the most comprehensive clearinghouse for information about persons of African ancestry. Worth a peek.

[Georgia Tech Black Graduate Students Association]

Comment	**UVote**
	http://www.uvote.com/
	Major issues confronting the United States are presented with possible solutions that have been proposed by politicians and "experts." Vote on those solutions you believe most likely to effectively solve the specified problem. Download the questions and results to compare class results on the poll. A rather thoughtful set of options is presented for each problem being studied.
	[UWSA Santa Clara Co., CA Chapter]
Comment	**War, Peace and Security Guide**
	http://www.cfcsc.dnd.ca/links/
	Over 6,000 links provide information on the armed forces of the world, current world "hot spots," international relations, disarmament efforts, peacekeeping missions, and military science, history, and biography. Links to other Canadian government offices are also included. Nothing fancy, but thorough coverage of resources related to peace and security.
	[Canadian Forces College, Department of National Defence, Canada]
Comment	**Washington International Magazine**
	http://www.washintl.com/wi/index.html?
	Although a commercial site, this online periodical does provide engaging material on world events, particularly the diplomatic corps. Its travel section includes many intriguing off-the-beaten-path locations not often covered in traditional travel magazines.
	[GlobeScope Internet Services]
Comment	**Washington Post—Talk Central**
	http://www.washingtonpost.com/wp-srv/talk/front.htm
	Discussion of national and international news events.
	[*Washington Post*]

ONLINE NEWSPAPERS

Comment	**Asahi News** http://www.asahi.com/english/english.html The English language text-only edition of Toyko's newspaper reports on news of Japan, the region, and the world. [Asahi Shimbun]
Comment	**Chicago Tribune** http://www.chicago.tribune.com/ An alternative view of current happenings. Attractive layout, user-friendly connections. [Chicago Tribune]
Comment	**Christian Science Monitor** http://www.csmonitor.com/ Hourly newscasts are offered 24 hours a day, Monday through Friday via Monitor Radio (via RealAudio). Continuous Associated Press news summaries are provided through this excellent resource. The quality of its Web site is equal to the high standards of its paper edition. Very functional layout; very user- friendly navigation; very professional, attractive graphics. [Christian Science Monitor]
Comment	**CNN Interactive** http://www.cnn.com/ Around-the-clock news updates are presented in a user-friendly, appealing Web site. The "Pager" function permits automatic updates on news items every 30 minutes. Some stories feature optional QuickTime movie clips. [Cable News Network, Inc.]
Comment	**Daily News** http://www.middlebury.edu/~gferguso/news.html

A+

A master listing of online editions of newspapers from everywhere in the world except the U.S. and Canada. It includes hundreds of English and non-English editions of papers from virtually every country. Updated frequently. Great source for learning different perspectives on current events.

[Gregory Ferguson-Cradler]

Comment

The Hindu

http://www.webpage.com/hindu/today/index.html

The online edition of India's national newspaper includes national, regional, and international news and a searchable archive.

[The Hindu and Paralogic Corporation]

Comment

HomeTown Free-Press

http://emporium.turnpike.net/~walk/hometown/fl.htm

Check this site for links to over 1,000 local newspapers and radio/television stations arranged by state.

[MicroNiche Publishing]

Comment

India World

http://indiaworld.com/open/index.html

News and views from India. Also provides a link to *India Abroad*, the United States' largest Indian-American newpaper.

[ASAP Solutions, Inc.]

Comment

Japan Times

http://www.japantimes.co.jp/

Online English edition of this Japanese newspaper provides coverage of the news of Japan and a different perspective on world events. Although the daily news reports are current, some of the background features are a month old or even older.

Comment	**Jerusalem Post Internet Edition** http://www.jpost.co.il/ Get a different perspective on world and Middle East news. A searchable archive of past issues is also available online.
Comment	**Nando Times** http://www.nando.net/welcome.html Updated throughout the day, this engaging electronic news site provides thorough coverage of U.S. and world news. The Nando News Watcher application can use your news browser to automatically download customized news reports, including only the topics you select. A special feature alerts you immediately if specified keywords should appear in any headlines. [McClatchy New Media Co.]
Comment	**New York Times** http://www.nytimes.com/info/contents/textpath.html View major portions of daily issues of the *New York Times*. Excellent graphics and easy-to-use index. Requires free registration of a username and password for access. [*New York Times*]
Comment	**Newspaper and Current Periodical Reading Room** http://lcweb.loc.gov/global/ncp/ncp.html Take a Cyberstroll through the Library of Congress Newspaper and Current Periodical Reading Room and browse through approximately 1,800 full-text journals. [Library of Congress]
Comment	**Newspapers in Education Online** http://detnews.com/nie/index.html A valuable source for lesson plans incorporating newspapers. Past issues are archived. Also includes general suggestions on using newpapers in the school. [*The Detroit News*]

A+

Comment	**The Newsroom** http://www.auburn.edu/~vestmon/news.html Check this gateway to a variety of news periodicals for up-to-the-minute reports on world events. The archive of current feature news stories is most useful for tracking stories. [Auburn University]
Comment	**San Francisco Chronicle** http://www.sfgate.com/ Free registration to "FishWrap" allows users to customize the newspaper they receive when they log in the next time. Check here for a great glimpse at the future for online newspapers. The "Personal Finance" section is particularly outstanding.
Comment	**USA Today** http://www.usatoday.com/ Online version of the first national daily newspaper. Its news, money, and life sections are filled with a broad array of timely articles. Provides useful links to sites related to most stories. [*USA Today*]
Comment	**Washington Post** http://www.washingtonpost.com/ With free registration receive a weekly e-mail update of "What's New." "Today's Top News" is updated 24 hours a day. [*Washington Post*]
Comment	**Washington Times** http://www.washtimes.com/fullindex/fullindex.html One of the first places to check for news on political developments. [*Washington Times*]

A+

A+

ELECTRONIC MAILING LISTS: CURRENT EVENTS

Many electronic mailing lists focus on topics of interest to sociology teachers and students. It is easy to subscribe. For example, to subscribe to the mailing list AFRICA-N providing African news and information:

Send an e-mail message to: LISTSERV@VM.UTCC.UTORONTO.EDU

Usually it is best to leave the "Subject" line blank. If your e-mail software requires something in the subject line, simply type a period.

Enter the message: subscribe AFRICA-N <your name>

The format for the message is: subscribe <List_Name> <Your_Full_Name>

Africa-N
African news and information
E-mail to: LISTSERV@VM.UTCC.UTORONTO.EDU

Afriqnews
African news service
E-mail to: LISTSERV@ATHENA.MIT.EDU

AIDS
AIDS discussion
E-mail to: RUTVM1.RUTGERS.EDU

Ascar-L
Canadian-American relations
E-mail to: ASCAR-L-REQUEST@QUCDN.QUEEN.CA

Balt-L
Baltic Republics forum
E-mail to: LISTSERV@UBVM.CC.BUFFALO.EDU

C-News
Conservative perspective on U.S. and world events
E-mail to: MAJORDOMO@WORLD.STD.COM

Canalc
Latin American and Caribbean events and culture
E-mail to: LISTSERV@VM1.YORKU.CA

China-NN
News of China
E-mail to: LISTSERV@UTARLVM1.UTA.EDU

Cndub-L
China news digest
E-mail to: LISTSERV@UBVM.CC.BUFFALO.EDU

Cuba-L
News and discussion of Cuba
E-mail to: LISTSERV@UNMVMA.UNM.EDU

Current
Current events forum
E-mail to: CURRENT-REQUEST@TOMAHAWK.WELCH.JHU.EDU

Defsec
Defense and security network
E-mail to: LISTSERV@CC1.KULEUVEN.AC.BE

Disarm-L
Disarmament issues
E-mail to: LISTSERV@UACSC2.ALBANY.EDU

Eca-L
Focus on Eastern Europe and the former Soviet Union
E-mail to: LISTSERV@GSUVM1.GSU.EDU

Femisa
Gender issues, feminism
E-mail to: LISTSERV@CSF.COLORADO.EDU

Firearms-Politics
Firearms legislation forum
E-mail to: FIREARMS-POLITICS-REQUEST@CS.CMU.EDU

Get-Online
Central Europe news digest
E-mail to: MAJORDOMO@EUNET.CZ

GPACS
Global peace and conflict forum
E-mail to: LISTSERV@UCI.EDU

IPM_L
Tehran news reports and analysis
E-mail to: LISTSERV@IREARN.BITNET

Ireland

Ireland news and discussion

E-mail to: LISTSERV@RUTVM1.RUTGERS.EDU

IRL-POL

Irish political issues

E-mail to: LISTSERV@RUTVM1.RUTGERS.EDU

Kalimba

Black/African culture and contemporary issues

E-mail to: LISTSERV@CASBAH.ACNS.NWU.EDU

Natodata

NATO reports and press releases

E-mail to: LISTSERV@CC1.KULEUVEN.AC.BE

News-Digest

Democratic party news digest

E-mail to: MAJORDOMO@DEMOCRATS.ORG

Newsflash

News of the Mideast

E-mail to: LISTSERV@ISRAEL.NYSERNET.ORG

Omri

News of the former Soviet Union and East European nations

E-mail to: LISTSERV@UBVM.CC.BUFFALO.EDU

Pacific

News of events in the Pacific

E-mail to: LISTSERV@BRUFPB.BITNET

Peace

Forum on peace issues and initiatives

E-mail to: LISTSERV@CSF.COLORADO.EDU

Talkback

News exchange and discussion for kids

E-mail to: LISTSERV@SJUVM.STJOHNS.EDU

UN-News

United Nations news digest

E-mail to: LISTSERV@UNMVMA.UNM.EDU

Newsgroups: Current Events

alt.current-events.usa	Current events in the U.S.
alt.disasters.misc	Firsthand accounts and news bulletins of natural disasters clari.world.asia.india
alt.journalism.criticism	Discussion of the news media practices
alt.politics.ec	Politics of the European Community
alt.politics.europe	Political issues in Europe
alt.politics.org.un	Political issues related the the United Nations
americast.usa-today.news	"News" section of *USA Today* clari.world.asia.india
misc.activism.progressive	Articles on activist politics
talk.politics.china	China's political issues
talk.politics.european-union	Issues related to the European Union
talk.politics.mideast	Discussion of Middle Eastern politics
uk.politics	Politics of the United Kingdom

Appendix

- ▲ ONLINE BEGINNER'S GUIDES TO USING THE INTERNET
- ▲ BOOKS ON USING THE INTERNET
- ▲ GLOSSARY OF COMMON INTERNET TERMS
- ▲ INTERNET SLANG AND CONVENTIONS

ONLINE BEGINNER'S GUIDES TO USING THE INTERNET

Any of these online guides should prove helpful for beginners, as well as for advanced users:

Comment	**Cyber Course** http://www.newbie.net/CyberCourse/ This free online training workshop is well written and presented in an easy-to-use, attractive design. Lessons are presented in modules which can be completed individually as time permits. "Newbies" should start with the Internet Orientation section. Splendid, but large graphics could take some time loading if less than a 14,400 modem is used. Persons with only e-mail access to the Internet can work on the course materials by sending an empty e-mail message to: CyberCourse-by-email@newbie.net. Course modules will be sent through the user's e-mail account. [NewbieNET International, Inc.]
Comment	**EFF's (Extended) Guide to the Internet** http://www.cosy.sbg.ac.at/doc/eegtti/ The online version of a book, *Adam Gaffin's EFF's (Extended) Guide to the Internet (formerly the Big Dummy's Guide to the Internet)*, is one of the oldest and most complete tutorials on using the Internet. You can download the whole book or just call up the sections you want to read online. The site is frequently updated. [The Electronic Frontier Foundation (EFF) and Apple Computer, Inc.]
Comment	**Exploring the World-Wide Web** http://www.gactr.uga.edu/exploring/toc.html Nothing fancy, but a good, concise description of the Internet, the World Wide Web and using Netscape Navigator. [University of Georgia Center for Continuing Education]
Comment	**Global Village's Internet Tour** http://www.globalvillage.com/gcweb/tour.html An easy-to-use, self-pacing tutorial moves you through "A Day on the Internet." The guide leads the user through var-

ious tasks which can be completed on the Internet, such as researching accounting software, or finding a government document. Cute, but quick-loading graphics enhance the presentation.

[Global Village Communication, Inc.]

Interactive Guide to the Internet

Comment

http://www.sierramm.com/smpnet.html

Windows users can download this file and install it on their computer to use at their leisure. Full directions are provided for downloading, installing and operating the program. The file should take about eight minutes to download on a 28.8-kbs modem. Minimal requirements for operation: a 386 IBM PC compatible computer and Microsoft Windows 3.1 or greater.

[Sierra Multimedia Productions of Northern Virginia]

Internet 101

Comment

http://www.sisna.com/users/scotting/101/internet101.html

All teachers and parents should read the section on "Safe Surfing" for guidelines to helping students avoid unsavory characters on the Internet. Included is an excellent list of "blocking" software for preventing access to unsuitable content. An excellent tutorial with sharp graphics. Very professionally done. A weekly online newsletter supplies additional tips and tricks.

[Scott Cottingham]

Internet Help Desk

Comment

http://w3.one.net/~alward/

What does a "Socket is not connected" message mean? Check this informative site for help in troubleshooting and finding answers to Internet-related questions. Lots of useful stuff here.

[Amy L. Ward]

Internet Starter Kit

Comment

http://www.mcp.com/hayden/iskm/book.html

Check this site for free online Macintosh and Windows editions of Adam Engst's best-selling book, *Internet Starter Kit*.

This exceptional guide contains all you need to become net-wise, and the price is right.

[Hayden Books and Adam C. Engst]

Internet Tour Bus

Comment

http://csbh.mhv.net/~bobrankin/tourbus/

This creative resource touts itself as "a virtual tour of the best of the Internet, delivered by e-mail to over 80,000 people in 120 countries." Access its home page using the above URL address to obtain information on how to subscribe to its Listserv. (Don't worry if you don't yet know about Listservs.) Very user-friendly.

[Patrick Douglas Crispen and Bob Rankin]

Learn the Net

Comment

http://www.learnthenet.com/

This colorful, one-stop workshop provides a large amount of well-organized, well-written information for both beginners and advanced users of the Internet.

[Paradesa Media]

Patrick Crispen's Internet Roadmap

Comment

http://www.brandonu.ca/~ennsnr/Resources/Roadmap/Welcome.html

This online tutorial features 27 lessons designed to be completed over a six-week period. Its plain text format makes this a good choice for graphically impaired computers.

[Neil Enns]

Zen and the Art of the Internet

Comment

http://www.cs.indiana.edu/docproject/zen/zen-1.0.html

An online version of Kehoe's 1992 edition of *Zen and the Art of the Internet: A Beginner's Guide to the Internet*. Though it is a bit dated, this Internet "classic" contains much useful content.

[Brendan P. Kehoe]

BOOKS ON USING THE INTERNET

Bock, W. (1996). *Getting on the information superhighway*. Menlo Park, CA: Crisp Publications.

Crumlish, C. (1996). *The Internet for busy people*. Berkeley: Osborne/McGraw-Hill.

Engst, A. C. (1996). *Internet starter kit for Macintosh*. 4th ed. Hayden.

Falk, B. (1994). *The Internet roadmap*. 2nd ed. San Francisco: Sybex.

Gralla, P. (1996). *How the Internet works: All new edition*. Emeryville, CA: Ziff-Davis Press.

Hahn, H. (1996). *The Internet complete reference*. 2nd ed. Berkeley: Osborne/McGraw-Hill.

Harnack, A. & Kleppinger, E. (1997). *Online!: A reference guide to using Internet sources*. New York: St. Martin's.

Levine, J. R. , Baroudi, C. & Young, M. L. (1996). *The Internet for dummies*. 3rd ed. Foster City, CA: IDG Books Worldwide.

Lumpkin, J. B. & Durnbaugh, S. B. (1995). *Getting started with the Internet*. New York: John Wiley.

Pfaffenberger, B. (1995). *World Wide Web Bible*. New York: MIS Press.

Salkind, N. J. (1996). *Hands-on Internet for Windows*. Danvers, MA: Boyd & Fraser.

Stout, R. (1996). *The World Wide Web complete reference*. Berkeley: Osborne/McGraw-Hill.

GLOSSARY OF COMMON INTERNET TERMS

Backbone   High-speed line or network that interconnects other networks.

Baud   The number of bits a modem can send or receive per second.

Bookmark   Web browser feature which enables you to save frequently accessed links in a bookmark file, rather than having to enter the URL manually each time.

BPS (Bits Per Second)   Speed at which data is transmitted. A 14.4 modem can move 14,400 bits per second.

Browser   Software application that facilitates viewing various kinds of World Wide Web resources. The most common ones are Netscape and Microsoft Explorer.

Cyberspace   Generally meaning the Internet. First used by William Gibson, author of the novel "Neuromancer."

Reading Domain Suffixes

The following are the approved online tags for domain addresses:

.arts	cultural groups
.com	a commercial entity
.edu	educational institution
.firm	businesses or firms
.gov	governmental bodies
.info	information services
.mil	military organization
.net	network entity
.nom	individuals
.org	non-profit group
.rec	recreational or entertainment activities
.store	businesses offering goods

Domain Name   The unique address that identifies an Internet site.

Download   To transfer files from one computer to another, generally by FTP (File Transfer Protocol) on the Internet.

E-mail (Electronic Mail)   Messages sent from one person to one or more other computers. May also refer to the method of transmitting these messages (e.g., "Send it to me by e-mail.").

Encryption   Encoding transmitted data for security.

Ezines   Electronic magazines.

FAQ (Frequently Asked Questions)   Documents that list and answer the most commonly asked questions on a subject. Most newsgroups maintain a file of FAQ's. It is a good idea to read these before submitting your own questions.

Finger   An Internet software tool for finding people at other Internet sites.

FTP (File Transfer Protocol)   Commonly used method for transferring files between two Internet sites. FTP is a procedure for logging in to another Internet site to retrieve or send files. Some Internet browsers like Netscape now do this internally.

GIF (Graphics Interchange Format) A universal format which facilitates transmitting and viewing graphic images. Software incorporating a GIF viewer is needed to view GIF files.

Home page/Homepage The main Web page for a Web site used as a starting point for navigating the files at that site.

Host Any computer on a network that acts as a server.

HTML (HyperText Markup Language) The coded language used to create Hypertext World Wide Web documents.

HTTP (HyperText Transport Protocol) The Internet standard for transmitting hypertext files across the World Wide Web.

Hyperlink A highlighted image or word on a Web page that, when clicked, is instantaneously connected to another Internet resource.

Hypertext Text that contains links to other documents, permitting nonlinear use of a collection of documents.

Internet The global collection of interconnected networks that all use the TCP/IP protocols.

Internet service provider A company that provides Internet accounts for individuals and organizations.

Kilobyte One thousand bytes. (Technically it is really 1,024 bytes.)

Listserv Program that automatically receives, sorts, and redistributes messages on a maillist server.

Mailing List/Maillist A discussion forum where participants with a common interest subscribe to a list and receive messages by e-mail. An e-mail message sent to one address is copied and sent to all of the other subscribers of the mailing list.

Megabyte One million bytes; a thousand kilobytes.

Modem (MOdulator, DEModulator) An electronic device that transmits messages typed into a computer over a phone line to other computers connected to the phone line.

Netscape One of the top World Wide Web browsers.

Network A connection of two or more computers together enabling them to share resources.

Newsgroup Discussion groups on USENET.

Newsreader Software that enables you to read and respond to newsgroup messages.

PPP (Point to Point Protocol) A fast, reliable method for using a regular telephone line and a modem to connect to the Internet.

Real-time chat An Internet function where live conversations can be carried on between two or more persons by typing on a computer terminal.

Search engine   Internet software that helps users search the millions of documents for specific items of interest. Usually conducted by typing keywords into an online form.

Server   A host computer, or a software package, that provides a specific kind of service (such as e-mail) to software running on other computers.

TCP/IP (Transmission Control Protocol/Internet Protocol)   A set of protocols that enable different types of computers to communicate with each other.

Under construction   Used to indicate that a WWW site is still being developed; often accompanied by a small graphic of a person using a shovel.

Upload   To move data from your computer to another. Opposite of download.

URL (Uniform Resource Locator)   The address of any resource on the Internet that is part of the World Wide Web; similar to a library book call number.

USENET   A set of discussion groups permitting individuals to post messages to all participants. Currently, there are over 14,000 discussion areas called newsgroups.

Web   The World Wide Web.

Webmaster   The individual responsible for maintaining a Web site.

World Wide Web/WWW   The universe of hypertext servers which enable text, graphics, sound file to be mixed together.

INTERNET SLANG AND CONVENTIONS

In communicating through e-mail and newsgroups, short-hand sets of abbreviations, slang, and keyboard pictures (emoticons) have emerged. Without some understanding of these, many e-mail messages will appear confusing and strange. Some of the more common ones are listed here.

AFAIK   As far as I know.

BTW   By the way.

Emoticon   A typed symbol used to communicate emotions via the Internet. Examples: :) "grin"   :-) "smile"

CYA   See You Around.

Flame   An angry response which puts down another, sometimes in a crude, blunt fashion. Expect some of these if you violate netiquette.

Flame War   A heated, derogatory exchange between two online discussion participants, becoming more crass and personal than based upon reasoned positions.

Common Emoticons

:-)	happy, funny
:-(	sad, angry
:-/	skeptical
::-)	user wears glasses.
:>	What?
:,(	crying.
:-O	oops
:-D	laughing person
;-)	winking

Freeware Free software downloadable on the Internet that may be redistributed.

FYA For your amusement.

Hotlist A list of frequently used URLs.

HTH Hope This Helps.

IMHO In My Humble Opinion; a shorthand notation preceding an online comment which is probably going to be an arguable assertion.

IOW In Other Words.

Lurking Reading newsgroup discussions without actively participating.

MOTD Message Of The Day.

Mouse Potato A person who spends excessive time at the computer.

Netiquette The etiquette expected of Internet users.

Netizen A citizen of the Internet; Internet user.

Newbie A novice; someone just starting to use the Internet.

OTOH On The Other Hand.

ONNA Oh No, Not Again.

POV Point Of View.

PPL People.

RTM Read The Manual; usually a sarcastic put-down.

Shareware   Software that may be tried before deciding to purchase. Users planning to continue using the program are expected to pay a registration fee. Some vendors provide documentation, technical support, and possible updated versions to those who register.

Spam/Spamming   To inappropriately use e-mail or a mailing list by posting a message to a large number of people who did not request it; to create "junk e-mail." Blatantly commercial pitches are particularly frowned upon.

Surf   To browse for information through World Wide Web jumping among hypertext links.

TIA   Thanks In Advance.

TTTT   To Tell The Truth.

Webzine   Magazine on the Internet.